Political Control of the Economy

Political Control of
the Economy

Edward R. Tufte

Princeton University Press, Princeton, New Jersey

Library of Congress Cataloging in Publication Data will be
found on the last printed page of this book
This book has been composed in Linotype Times Roman
Clothbound editions of Princeton University Press books
are printed on acid-free paper, and binding materials
are chosen for strength and durability
Printed in the United States of America by
Princeton University Press, Princeton, New Jersey

TO MY PARENTS
Edward E. Tufte
and
Virginia James Tufte

Contents

Preface

To understand the economic policies and the economic performances of the world's capitalist democracies, it is necessary to have a political theory of economic policy. The development of such a theory requires evidence demonstrating
that political life affects economic outcomes in a regular, persistent fashion. Should the impact of politics on economic life
be only through occasional random shocks—a new president
or prime minister with a new policy, an oil embargo, a war
—then the possibility of developing a political theory of economic policy would be slight. In this book, consequently, I
seek to show how certain political variables determine
macroeconomic outcomes in a systematic and predictable
way. In particular, I provide evidence demonstrating the role
of elections and political parties in deciding who gets what,
when, and how in the economic arena.

A verifiable political theory of economic policy is a delight
in and of itself, relevant and important on its own terms
because its key elements—elections, political parties, and
macroeconomic performance—are relevant and important.
A political analysis of economic outcomes has additional interest, however, because it helps to clarify a largely unana-
lyzed aspect of contemporary democratic theory: how can
the citizens of a large capitalist country control macroeconomic outcomes? And, further, to what extent should citizens
and their political leaders control what many economists argue are the complex technical and managerial aspects of
economic policy?

This book describes the interplay between politics and
macroeconomics in the United States and other capitalist
democracies. The point is more than the banal one that the

polity and the economy have something to do with one another. Rather my purposes are to show how things work, to find specific links between political and economic life, and to provide quantitative estimates of the potency of those links when possible.

The explanations developed here grow from the premise that the politicians who make economic policy operate under conditions of political competition. The simple fact of competition, especially when that competition is informed by political ideology, explains a great deal of what goes on in the political world and, I argue, in important parts of the economic world also. Because of their general premises, the results apply to all economically developed democracies.

Many of the empirical findings reported here are new; others are extensions of past work. Some of the detailed content of the theory is fresh, although the fundamental idea that politics has much to do with deciding economic outcomes has a long and vital tradition.

Data sources and materials relating to data error structure are reported in the Appendix.

I am indebted to many for their help with this book. I remember gratefully:

For leave and research support during several academic years, the Center for Advanced Study in the Behavioral Sciences, the John Simon Guggenheim Foundation, the Woodrow Wilson School of Princeton University, and Yale University.

For their help with data collection and analysis, Marge Cruise, Jan Juran, Michael Lytton, Alice Anne Navin, and Susan Spock.

For providing research advice and information about economic policy, John T. Bennett, Jr., Yoram Ben-Porath, William Branson, John P. Crecine, Michael R. Kagay, David W. MacNeill, Arthur H. Miller, William A. Niskanen, Arthur C. Okun, George Schultz, Daniel Shimshoni, Nancy Teeters, and Paul Volker.

For criticizing the manuscript and for their encouragement, Albert D. Biderman, Alan S. Blinder, Willem Buiter, Morris P. Fiorina, Edward J. Kane, Stanley Kelley, Jr., Gerald H. Kramer, Assar Lindbeck, Robert K. Merton, David Seidman, Eileen Shanahan, Donald E. Stokes, Dennis F. Thompson, Norman Uphoff, and Jack Walker.

For their persistence in seeing this enterprise through, my friends at Princeton University Press, Joanna Hitchcock and Sandy Thatcher.

For their inspiration and patient understanding, the late Judith Baskin Offer, Charles and Tanya Tufte, and Ellen Woodbury.

October 1977
Cheshire, Connecticut

Political Control of the Economy

1

The Electoral-Economic Cycle

A Government is not supported a hundredth part so much by the constant, uniform, quiet prosperity of the country as by those damned spurts which Pitt used to have just in the nick of time.

Brougham, 1814

The year 1972 ended with considerable forward momentum in economic activity. According to preliminary fourth quarter data, GNP rose by $32 billion, or at a seasonally adjusted rate of 11½ percent. . . . Judging from monthly indicators such as industrial production, the course of output was strongly upward through the quarter.

*Annual Report of the Council
of Economic Advisers, 1973*

Some circumstantial evidence is very strong, as when you find a trout in the milk.

Henry David Thoreau

The government of a modern democratic country exerts very substantial control over the pace of national economic life and the distribution of economic benefits. While it cannot always dilute the consequences of exogenous shocks, reduce unemployment or inflation below certain levels, or protect its citizens from the vicissitudes of world markets, the government's control over spending, taxes, transfers, money stock, and the like enables it to direct the short-run course of the economy to a significant degree. We need not, therefore, be as agnostic as the Council of Economic Advisers' 1973 *Report* with respect to the causes of "considerable forward momentum in economic activity"—in this case, an 11.5 percent growth rate—occurring in the fourth quarter of a presidential election year. It is hardly a novel hypothesis that an incumbent administration, while operating within political and economic constraints and limited by the usual uncertain-

3

ties in successfully implementing economic policy, may manipulate the short-run course of the national economy in order to improve its party's standing in upcoming elections and to repay past political debts. In particular, incumbents may seek to determine the *location* and the *timing* of economic benefits in promoting the fortunes of their party and friends.

The hypothesis of an electoral-economic cycle is nearly integrated into the folklore of capitalist democracies; political motives are regularly attributed to economic policies in election years. Furthermore, the formal possibilities for such a cycle have been developed in some technical detail in economic analysis.[1] As is often the case with folklore and with economic theory, however, little empirical evidence bearing on the question is available. A few case studies of a single country over a short period of time have found some evidence for the acceleration of the national economy in an election year, but these studies leave one wondering if other

[1] The three fundamental papers, each with a very different perspective on political economics, are M. Kalecki, "Political Aspects of Full Employment," *Political Quarterly*, 14 (October-December 1943), 322-331; William D. Nordhaus, "The Political Business Cycle," *Review of Economic Studies*, 42 (April 1975), 169-190; and Assar Lindbeck, "Stabilization Policy in Open Economies with Endogenous Politicians," *American Economic Review*, 66 (May 1976), 1-19. Other major developments are found in C.A.E. Goodhart and R. J. Bhansali, "Political Economy," *Political Studies*, 18 (March 1970), 43-106; W. Miller and M. Mackie, "The Electoral Cycle and the Asymmetry of Government and Opposition Popularity," *Political Studies*, 21 (September 1973), 263-279; C. Duncan MacRae, "A Political Model of the Business Cycle," working paper, December 1971, The Urban Institute, Washington, D.C.; Raford Boddy and James Crotty, "Class Conflict and Macro-Policy: The Political Business Cycle," *Review of Radical Political Economics*, 7 (Spring 1975), 1-19; and the many papers of Frey and his co-workers, including Bruno S. Frey and Friedrich Schneider, "On the Modelling of Politico-Economic Interdependence," *European Journal of Political Research*, 3 (1975), 339-360. Suggestions for further research are developed in Ryan C. Amacher, William J. Boyes, Thomas Deaton, and Robert D. Tollison, "The Political Business Cycle: A Review of Theoretical and Empirical Evidence," manuscript, 1977.

times or places would testify differently. After all, no investigators have sought to find the *lack* of a link between economic policy and elections. The only analysis comparing a number of countries, after a casual review of unemployment data, yielded very mixed findings: "The overall results indicate that for the entire period a political cycle seems to be implausible as a description for Australia, Canada, Japan, and the UK. Some modest indications of a political cycle appear for France and Sweden. For three countries—Germany, New Zealand and the United States—the coincidence of business and political cycles is very marked."[2] In short, virtually no evidence confirming even the existence of an electoral-economic cycle is at hand, let alone considerations on its measurement, causes, and consequences. The absence of evidence, however, is not convincing evidence of absence.

Let us begin by seeking a motive, an initiating cause for an electoral-economic cycle. It is obvious enough: incumbent politicians desire re-election and they believe that a booming pre-election economy will help to achieve it.

The Economic Theory of Elections Held by Politicians and Their Economic Advisers

It has been a political commonplace since the massive political realignment growing out of the Great Depression that the performance of the economy affects the electoral fate of the dominant incumbent party. Ample evidence confirms that politicians and high-level economic advisers appreciate what they see as an economic fact of political life. At hand is the rueful testimony of politicians and the more self-important pronouncements of their economic advisers that short-run economic fluctuations are very important politically. Walter Heller, the chairman of the Council of Economic Advisers from 1961 to 1964, wrote:

[2] Nordhaus, "Political Business Cycle," p. 186. Similar mixed results are reported in Martin Paldam, "Is There an Electional Cycle? A Comparative Study of National Accounts," Institute of Economics, University of Aarhus, Denmark, 1977, no. 8.

5

As a political leader, President Johnson has found in modern economic policy an instrument that serves him well in giving form and substance to the stuff of which his dreams for America are made, in molding and holding a democratic consensus, and in giving that consensus a capital "D" in national elections. That the chill of recession may have tipped the Presidential election in 1960, and that the bloom of prosperity boosted the margin of victory in 1964, is widely acknowledged, especially by the defeated candidates.[3]

Richard Nixon expressed a similar view in *Six Crises*:

I knew from bitter experience how, in both 1954 and 1958, slumps which hit bottom early in October contributed to substantial Republican losses in the House and Senate. The power of the "pocket-book" issue was shown more clearly perhaps in 1958 than in any off-year election in history. On the international front, the Administration had had one of its best years. . . . Yet, the economic dip in October was obviously uppermost in the people's minds when they went to the polls. They completely rejected the President's appeal for the election of Republicans to the House and Senate.[4]

And, with regard to the 1960 presidential contest, Nixon wrote:

Unfortunately, Arthur Burns turned out to be a good prophet. The bottom of the 1960 dip did come in October and the economy started to move up in November—after it was too late to affect the election returns. In October, usually a month of rising employment, the jobless rolls increased by 452,000. All the speeches, television broadcasts, and precinct work in the world could not counteract that one hard fact.[5]

[3] Walter W. Heller, *New Dimensions of Political Economy* (Cambridge, Mass.: Harvard University Press, 1966), p. 12.

[4] Richard M. Nixon, *Six Crises* (Garden City, N.Y.: Doubleday, 1962), p. 309.

[5] Ibid., pp. 310-311.

The matter was put most bluntly in a memorandum that Paul Samuelson wrote to President Kennedy and the Council of Economic Advisers:

> When my grandchildren ask me: "Daddy, what did you do for the New Frontier?", I shall sadly reply: "I kept telling them down at the office, in December, January, *and* April that, WHAT THIS COUNTRY NEEDS IS AN ACROSS THE BOARD RISE IN DISPOSABLE INCOME TO LOWER THE LEVEL OF UNEMPLOYMENT, SPEED UP THE RECOVERY AND THE RETURN TO HEALTHY GROWTH, PROMOTE CAPITAL FORMATION AND THE GENERAL WELFARE, INSURE DOMESTIC TRANQUILITY AND THE TRIUMPH OF THE DEMOCRATIC PARTY AT THE POLLS."[6]

A month before the 1976 presidential election, L. William Seidman, a top economic adviser and confidant of President Ford, commented on the slight downturn in the leading economic indicators for September: ". . . the economic issue could be important. It had been one of the strongest things we had going for us. When things turn sluggish, we lose some of the advantage."[7] A week before the election, Seidman again expressed his concern about the fall pause in the economy: "I think Mr. Ford's chances for re-election are very good. As for the economic lull, we considered the use of stimulus to make sure we didn't have a low third quarter, but the President didn't want anything to do with a short-term view."[8]

News reports, memoirs, and internal political documents abound with similar analyses by politicians, their economic advisers, and journalists.[9] In fact, since the 1930s only one

[6] Paul Samuelson, "Memorandum for the President and the Council of Economic Advisers: That 'April Second Look' at the Economy," March 21, 1961 (John F. Kennedy Presidential Library).

[7] Hobart Rowen, "Ford Aide Sees Lag in GNP Aiding Carter," *Washington Post*, October 6, 1976, p. A17.

[8] Vartanig G. Vartan, "Seidman Expects Leveling in Leading Economic Index: Ford Adviser Says Pause Is Now Lull," *New York Times*, October 26, 1976, p. 51.

[9] The best guides are Herbert Stein, *The Fiscal Revolution in*

administration has seemingly taken exception to the hypothesis that economic growth and stimulative fiscal policy are the important things politically. President Eisenhower and most of his cabinet officers (other than Richard Nixon), perhaps projecting their own ideological views on the electorate, felt that what voters wanted was a balanced federal budget—or, even better, a budget in surplus—and protection against inflation. But the belief in the political value of big budget surpluses and muted economic growth never took hold among politicians and economic policy-makers, particularly since they attributed the Republican losses of 1954, 1958, and 1960 to economic declines during those election years.[10]

America (Chicago: University of Chicago Press, 1969) and James L. Sundquist, *Politics and Policy: The Eisenhower, Kennedy, and Johnson Years* (Washington, D.C.: The Brookings Institution, 1968). For Britain, David Butler and Donald Stokes report: ". . . how deeply rooted in British politics is the idea that the Government is accountable for good and bad times. Popular acceptance of this idea means that the state of the economy has loomed large in the minds of all modern Prime Ministers as they pondered on the timing of a dissolution. And in the post-Keynesian era more than one government has been tempted to seek a favorable context for an election by expanding the economy, although dissolutions are more easily timed to coincide with expansion than the other way round" (*Political Change in Britain*, 2nd ed. [New York: St. Martin's Press, 1974], p. 369).

[10] Nixon pointed to economic downturns in the few months before the elections of 1954, 1958, and 1960 (*Six Crises*, pp. 309-312). Sundquist makes a similar point: "Three elections [1954, 1958, and 1960] had taught the politicians that they *must* respond to the issue of unemployment whenever it appears. In a more positive sense, experience since 1964 had also taught them that a full employment economy provides the greater revenues from which the politicians' dreams are realized" (*Politics and Policy*, p. 56). And James Tobin sharpens the observation: "Recessions of course are politically dangerous, as Republican defeats in 1932, 1954, 1958, 1960—we might add 1970—indicate. But a first-derivative mentality is strong in American politics. Provided economic indicators are moving up, their level is secondary. Incidentally, politico-econometric studies of the influence of economic variables on elections confirm this instinctive feeling of politicians: the current growth rate of GNP counts for votes, but not the level of unemployment" (*The New Economics One Decade Older* [Princeton: Princeton University Press, 1974], p. 20).

The main propositions, in summary, of the politicians' theory of the impact of economic conditions on election outcomes emphasize short-run economic shifts:

1. Economic movements in the months immediately preceding an election can tip the balance and decide the outcome of an election.
2. The electorate rewards incumbents for prosperity and punishes them for recession.
3. Short-run spurts in economic growth in the months immediately preceding an election benefit incumbents.

What are the consequences of the politicians' economic theory of elections? Do incumbent administrations act on the theory and attempt to engineer election-year economic accelerations? Do macroeconomic fluctuations ride the electoral cycle? If so, what instruments of economic policy are deployed in election years?

The next two chapters answer these questions. My first concern is to show that electoral-economic cycles actually do exist.

ELECTORAL-ECONOMIC CYCLES IN 27 DEMOCRACIES

How is an electoral-economic cycle to be detected and measured? A whole range of economic indicators might be matched up with election dates in a shotgun search for correlations. Instead of cycle-searching through economic time-series, however, let us try to obtain some theoretical guidance to the electoral-economic cycle by considering the perspective of the incumbent administration on election-year economics. If the administration seeks a pre-election economic stimulation, it seems likely that the economic policy instruments involved must be easy to start up quickly and must yield clear and immediate economic benefits to a large number of voters—or at least to some specific large groups of voters if the benefits are targeted as well as timed. Increased transfer payments, tax cuts, and postponements in tax increases—all of which have a widespread impact and can be legislated and implemented quickly—are the policy instruments that come to mind. Election-year economics is probably not often a matter of sophisticated macroeconomic policy. The politicians' economic theory of election outcomes gives great weight to economic events in the months before the election; thus the politicians' strategy is to turn on the spigot surely and swiftly and fill the trough so that it counts with the electorate.

These considerations suggest that short-run fluctuations in real disposable income might be a good aggregate signal of the pre-election stimulation of the economy. Real disposable income, unlike other major aspects of aggregate economic performance (such as unemployment, inflation, or real growth), can be immediately and directly influenced by short-run government action through taxes and transfers with little uncertainty about the time lag between activation of the policy instruments and the resulting change in real disposable income. For example, a few days after increased social security or veterans checks are in the mail, real disposable personal income has increased. In fact, in normal economic times, taxes and transfers have more to do with determining real disposable income than whether the economy goes faster or slower. Changes in real disposable income, furthermore, have special political relevance: several studies have found that upswings in real disposable income per capita are highly correlated with greater electoral support for incumbents.[11]

It is appropriate to look at the rate of change in real disposable income in relation to elections in *all* the world's democratic countries. Earlier we saw evidence that U.S. politicians believed that pre-election prosperity would help them retain office when they sought re-election. No doubt similar beliefs—as well as the desire to be re-elected—animate members of the political elite in almost any democracy. Consequently, I assembled electoral and economic time-

[11] Gerald Kramer, "Short-Term Fluctuations in U.S. Voting Behavior, 1896-1964," *American Political Science Review*, 65 (March 1971), 131-143; and Edward R. Tufte, "Determinants of the Outcomes of Midterm Congressional Elections," *American Political Science Review*, 69 (September 1975), 812-826. Further evidence is discussed in Chapters 4 and 5 below.

series (election dates, disposable income, price changes, and population) for all 29 countries classified as "democracies" circa 1969—those nations with both widespread participation in free elections and an effective political opposition.[12] For 27 of the 29 (missing were Lebanon and Trinidad-Tobago), data sufficient to compute changes in real disposable income per capita for each year from 1961 to 1972 were found. Then the yearly acceleration-deceleration in real disposable income per capita was compared with the timing of elections in each of the 27 democracies.

The findings are clear. Evidence for an electoral-economic cycle was found in 19 of the 27 countries; in those 19, short-run accelerations in real disposable income per capita were more likely to occur in election years than in years without elections. Table 1-1 shows the results. Combining all the experience of the 27 countries over the period 1961-1972 reveals that real disposable income growth accelerated in 64 percent of all elections years ($N = 90$) compared to 49 percent of all the years without elections ($N = 205$). Furthermore, for those 19 countries whose economies ran faster than usual in election years, the effect was substantial: real disposable income growth accelerated in 77 percent of election years compared with 46 percent of years without elections.

The data in Table 1-1 provide only aggregate testimony; to convince ourselves that in *each* of the 19 individual countries a political-economic cycle occurs would require considerably more evidence—a longer data series, more detail about the structure of the cycle, and a deeper understanding of the politics of economic policy in the various democracies. The fundamental point of the aggregate evidence is that 70 percent of the countries showed some signs of a political business cycle.[13]

[12] The list is from Robert A. Dahl, *Polyarchy: Participation and Opposition* (New Haven: Yale University Press, 1971), pp. 231-248. The data sources for each table and figure are described in the the Appendix, "Data Sources," p. 155.

[13] Since election dates in these democracies are scattered over the years, the observed relationship between the occurrence of elections and short-run economic stimulation is not the artifactual product

11

TABLE 1-1

ELECTIONS AND ECONOMIC ACCELERATION, 27 DEMOCRACIES, 1961-1972

	Percentage of years in which rate of growth of real disposable income increased				Did acceleration in real income growth occur more often in election years compared to years without an election?
	Election years	N	Years without elections	N	
Australia	75%	4	29%	7	yes
Austria	25%	4	86%	7	no
Belgium	67%	3	63%	8	yes
Canada	100%	5	57%	7	yes
Chile	50%	2	44%	9	yes
Costa Rica	100%	2	50%	8	yes
Denmark	25%	4	43%	7	no
Finland	67%	3	50%	8	yes
France	60%	5	33%	6	yes
Germany	33%	3	38%	8	no
Iceland	33%	3	75%	8	no
India	50%	2	43%	7	yes
Ireland	67%	3	63%	8	yes
Israel	67%	3	50%	8	yes
Italy	33%	3	50%	8	no
Jamaica	100%	2	44%	9	yes
Japan	100%	4	29%	7	yes
Luxembourg	100%	2	56%	9	yes
Netherlands	50%	4	57%	7	no
New Zealand	75%	4	43%	7	yes
Norway	100%	2	33%	9	yes
Philippines	60%	5	67%	6	no
Sweden	67%	3	50%	8	yes
Switzerland	67%	3	50%	8	yes
United Kingdom	67%	3	38%	8	yes
United States	83%	6	40%	5	yes
Uruguay	33%	3	50%	8	no

A few countries have been studied more systematically. For Israel, Ben-Porath reports:

In following the timing of discrete policy decisions, one can observe a fairly consistent pattern. Thus, for example, of the seven devaluations that took place in the period [1952-1973], the closest that one ever came to preceding an election was eighteen months. (The eighth devaluation took place in November 1974 approximately three years before the next scheduled elections.) When a public committee recommended reducing income tax rates and imposing a value added tax the government proceeded to implement the first in April 1973, expecting elections in November 1973, but waited with the second.[14]

For the six parliamentary elections from 1952 to 1973, per capita annual consumption accelerated during the year before the election five out of six times; the average pre-election increase in consumption was 7.4 percent compared to 2.0 percent in the post-election periods. Similarly, per capita GNP increased a pre-election average of 7.9 percent as against a post-election 3.7 percent.

In the Philippines, the economy moved with the electoral cycle in a "biennial lurch" from 1957 to 1966 according to Averch, Koehler, and Denton. They sketch out a fairly complete pattern of political economics:

Although it is growing rapidly, the Philippine economy also appears to be rather unstable. At least until 1966, the reported rate of growth of real GNP alternately rose and fell in a two-year cycle. . . . The survey data . . . suggest that both politicians and voters perceive election strategy in terms of allocating public works, jobs, and var-

---

of common worldwide changes in economic conditions. At least such was the case in the 1960s. In Chapter 3, however, I shall present evidence for the increasing synchronization since 1970 of election timing in the major capitalist democracies.

[14] Yoram Ben-Porath, "The Years of Plenty and the Years of Famine—A Political Business Cycle?" *Kyklos*, 28 (1975), 400.

ious other payoffs to maximize votes . . . the unevenness we observe is in part the consequence of fiscal and monetary policies that work together to destabilize the economy. The instability does not reflect the impact of uncontrollable events but is built into the Philippine political system. As Philippine policymakers pursue and *achieve* their goals, they generate the cycles we have observed.[15]

The policy instrument implicated was the government budget: deficits were run in six straight election years and surpluses in the five intervening years.

The studies of Israel and the Philippines help shore up the wishy-washy results for these two countries recorded in Table 1-1. All the available material combined—the case studies of Israel and the Philippines, Nordhaus's report on the coincidence of unemployment and electoral cycles in Germany, New Zealand, and the United States, and, most importantly, the results of Table 1-1—yields evidence of electoral-economic cycles in 21 of the world's 27 democracies.[16]

[15] Harvey A. Averch, John E. Koehler, and Frank H. Denton, *The Matrix of Policy in the Philippines* (Princeton: Princeton University Press, 1971), pp. 95-96. The capital-intensive character of Philippine elections, election-stimulated inflation, and post-election retrenchment appear to have combined to produce both an unstable economy and unstable ruling coalitions. On this, see the excellent analysis in Thomas C. Nowak, "The Philippines before Martial Law: A Study in Politics and Administration," *American Political Science Review*, 71 (June 1977), 522-539.

[16] I investigated the possibility that electoral-economic cycles might be more likely to occur in countries having irregular election schedules, where the date of the election is set by the incumbent government. The cycle, however, appeared with nearly equal frequency in countries with flexible election dates and in countries with fixed dates. A more subtle possibility is that countries with non-periodic election dates have elections called at economic extremes, with the incumbent government seizing the opportunity for electoral gains in prosperous times and crumbling in times of economic crisis. The hypothesis is too subtle to test with the data of Table 1-1. For countries with non-periodic elections, the direction of the causal arrow must remain ambiguous: does a bouyant economy produce elections or does the prospect of elections produce stimulative economic

Chapter 3, dealing with the internationalization of the electoral-economic cycle, will present some additional comparative data. But for now let us look more carefully at the experience of the United States.

THE POLITICAL HISTORY OF REAL DISPOSABLE INCOME IN THE UNITED STATES

Incumbent administrations in postwar America have generally enjoyed quite a perky electoral-economic cycle. Figure 1-1 displays the path of yearly changes in real disposable income per capita in the United States since 1947. During the Truman, Kennedy, Johnson, Nixon, and Ford administrations, the short-run growth in real disposable income per capita tended to swing up in election years and drop down in odd-numbered years. The tie between elections and a quickening economy is a strong one: in those five administrations, real income growth accelerated in eight of eleven election years (73 percent) compared to only two of ten years (20 percent) without elections.

Things were different during the Eisenhower administration. Real income growth declined in every election year (1954, 1956, 1958, and 1960), but rose in three of the four intervening years without elections. Things were different because the economic goals and the evaluations of what was politically sound economic policy were different. The dominant political-economic goals of the Eisenhower presidency, unlike those of other postwar administrations, were the reduction of inflation and a balanced (and small) federal budget. These economic beliefs were initially reinforced by the election returns: Eisenhower read his landslide victory in 1952 as the voters' express approval of these goals and as the rejection of the Democratic focus on governmental

---

policies? Such questions, which depend among other things on the time horizons of politicians and how politicians perceive the time horizons of voters, pose difficult problems of model specification and estimation.

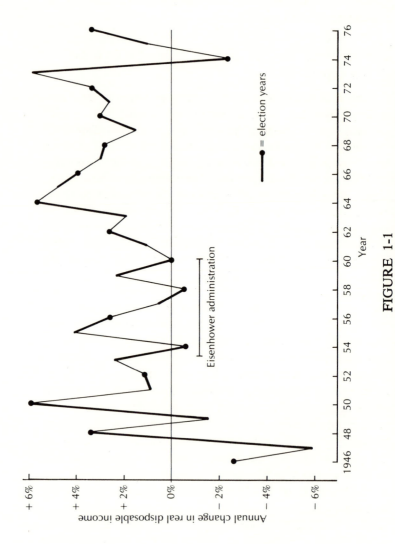

FIGURE 1-1

YEARLY CHANGES IN REAL DISPOSABLE INCOME PER CAPITA, 1946-1976

intervention to reduce unemployment. The Eisenhower administration memoirs, fiscal histories, and diaries—unlike those of any other postwar administration—bristle with determined statements on the need to avoid inflation and reduce the federal budget. Stimulative interventionist policies by the government were to be avoided because they ultimately stifled creative business initiative and because they served little purpose, since economic downturns and unemployment were seen as self-curing.[17] These doctrines held firm even in the face of the deep pre-election economic slump of 1958 and the Burns-Nixon proposal to the cabinet to stimulate the economy in the months before the 1960 election.[18] In fact, going into the elections of 1954, 1956, and 1960, the federal budget was less stimulative than in the previous odd-numbered years; for two of those election years, moreover, the federal budget was in surplus. Perhaps there was a political budget cycle.[19] That policy, if it was a policy, may have grown out of a conviction that voters cared

[17] Full details are in Stein, *Fiscal Revolution*, chapters 11-14, and Sundquist, *Politics and Policy*. See also Edward S. Flash, Jr., *Economic Advice and Presidential Leadership* (New York: Columbia University Press, 1965) and Eisenhower's memoirs *Mandate for Change* (Garden City, N.Y.: Doubleday, 1963) and *Waging Peace* (Garden City, N.Y.: Doubleday, 1965).

[18] See Eisenhower, *Waging Peace*, pp. 307-310; and Nixon, *Six Crises*, pp. 309-311.

[19] Evidence on this point is found in a letter from the Secretary of the Treasury, George M. Humphrey, to President Eisenhower on December 6, 1956 (Eisenhower Presidential Library):

> These are a few thoughts I hope you may have in mind as you think of the problem of the budget. The matter of timing is of very great importance as to both politics and economics.
>
> *As to politics:* I believe we can resist any major tax reductions this coming year provided there is a real prospect of an important tax reduction to be effective in 1958. . . .
>
> Barring a war, I think there will have to be a substantial general tax reduction sometime during the next four years and, politically, the best time to have it will be in 1958. If this occurs, we will be in approximately the same situation as in the past four years and the voters will actually have the benefit of a tax cut for a couple of years before the next Presidential election.

17

as strongly about a balanced federal budget as those who shaped economic policy. Certainly the economic outcomes differed; the results for all 15 election years from 1948 to 1976 were:[20]

	Number of election years in which growth in real disposable income	
	accelerated	decelerated
Eisenhower administration	0	4
Other administrations	8	3

The Eisenhower years demonstrated that when the administration's views on political economy changed the political-economic cycle also changed. Once a new administration came into office in 1961 with a contrary doctrine about what was politically important as far as the economy was concerned, the match of the ups and downs of real income growth to election years was restored.[21]

[20] The exact probability (via the hypergeometric distribution) of observing an outcome as extreme as that shown in the two-by-two table in the text, under the null hypothesis that there is no difference between the Eisenhower and the other administrations, is only 1/39 or about 0.026 (under the assumptions of fixed marginals and independence of observations). Consequently we reject either the null hypothesis or the assumptions. The Eisenhower case is bothersome, naturally raising questions about the selective use of evidence. It appears that the Eisenhower administration did make electoral cycle calculations in formulating its economic policies, but that other priorities—preventing inflation, limiting government intervention in the economy, seeking a budget surplus—were far more important than the all-out stimulation of the economy in election years. Given Eisenhower's assured re-election in 1956 and his quite limited devotion to the 1960 Nixon campaign, it is not surprising that ideological priorities in economic policy substituted for heating up the pre-election economy. Finally, in this chapter as well as the next two we shall see a great deal of additional evidence (mostly not dependent on the Eisenhower exclusion) that details the structure and content of the electoral-economic cycle.

[21] A sharp contrast between the two administrations is provided in Paul Samuelson, "Economic Policy for 1962," *Review of Eco-*

A FOUR-YEAR CYCLE IN UNEMPLOYMENT

Let us examine another indicator of economic well-being, the unemployment rate, in relation to the U.S. electoral cycle. Nordhaus found that unemployment has tended to reach a low point around election time in Germany, New Zealand, the United States, and perhaps France and Sweden.[22] Evidence for the United States is shown in Figure 1-2, where the path of monthly unemployment is centered around the schedule of presidential elections from 1948 to 1976. In the main, unemployment has bottomed out every fourth November.[23] Unemployment levels twelve to eighteen months before presidential elections have exceeded unemployment levels at election time in six of the last eight presidential elections. (If the planned economic targets from 1977 to 1980 are achieved, the score will be up to seven out of nine by 1980.[24])

---

nomics and Statistics, 44 (1962), 3-6; and in Seymour E. Harris, *The Economics of the Two Political Parties* (New York: Macmillan, 1962). See also Tobin, *The New Economics One Decade Older.*

[22] Nordhaus, "Political Business Cycle," p. 186. I have borrowed the arrangement for my Figure 1-2 from an unpublished draft of Nordhaus's paper.

[23] The unemployment rates reported here are seasonally adjusted, thereby removing (among other things) the normal downturn in unemployment (unadjusted) occurring in the fall of each year. Thus the actual, unadjusted unemployment rates would show a sharper pre-election improvement. This becomes an interesting issue in understanding how the electorate responds to pre-election economic changes: Do voters seasonally adjust? If not, then the normal autumn economic upswing benefits incumbents in those countries holding elections late in the year.

[24] In his press conference on November 16, 1976, President-elect Carter said: "We believe that we can get the unemployment rate down over a fairly long period of time—two, three or perhaps four years—to the 4 to 4½ percent figure before excessive inflation will be felt. But I will reveal my plans as they are evolved. They are not final enough now to discuss further" (*New York Times,* November 16, 1976, p. 32). Later, the 1980 unemployment goal became 4.75 percent. See James T. Wooten, "Carter Delay on Endorsing Bill Linked to 4% Unemployment Provision," *New York Times,* October 20, 1977, p. A12.

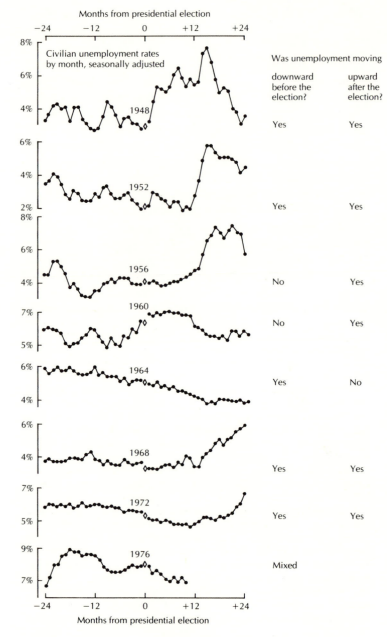

FIGURE 1-2
UNEMPLOYMENT RATES AND THE CYCLE OF PRESIDENTIAL ELECTIONS, 1946-1976

The elections during the Eisenhower administration, 1956 and 1960, are the only exceptions: while unemployment dipped slightly in 1956, everything was wrong, politically, with the pre- and post-election shifts in unemployment in 1960.

Omitting the two presidential elections taking place during the Eisenhower administration, the pre-election downturn in the unemployment rate in all the other postwar presidential elections is quite phenomenal:

—The unemployment rate in November 1948 was lower than in *all but five* of the preceding twenty-four months.

—The unemployment rate in November 1952 was lower than in *all but one* of the preceding twenty-four months.

—The unemployment rate in November 1964 was lower than in *all but two* of the preceding twenty-four months.

—The unemployment rate in November 1968 was lower than in *all* of the preceding twenty-four months.

—The unemployment rate in November 1972 was lower than in *all* of the preceding twenty-four months.

—The unemployment rate in November 1976 was lower than in *eleven* of the preceding twenty-four months.

Except in the Eisenhower years, the election-day unemployment rate has averaged about one percentage point below the rate twelve to eighteen months before the election and nearly two percentage points below the post-election unemployment rate twelve to eighteen months after the presidential election.

Presidential Elections in Relation to the Trade-Off between Inflation and Unemployment

Since 1946, the American economy has beaten the putative trade-off between inflation and unemployment—by having less of both—in only six years. Four of these six great economic successes were delivered in presidential election years.

The trade-off broke down in four other years when both inflation and unemployment increased. None of these failures took place in a presidential election year, although three of them—in 1946, 1970, and 1974—did occur at the time of off-year congressional elections.

Table 1-2 shows the joint inflation-unemployment movements in relation to presidential elections for all thirty-one years from 1946 to 1976. It is apparent that the way to defeat the trade-off between inflation and unemployment in the short-run is to hold a presidential election.

TABLE 1-2

INFLATION, UNEMPLOYMENT, AND PRESIDENTIAL ELECTIONS, 1946-1976

Yearly change in unemployment rate and inflation (real GNP deflator):	Presidential election years	All other years
less unemployment and less inflation	50%	9%
less unemployment, but more inflation	13	30
less inflation, but more unemployment	38	43
more inflation and more unemployment	0	17
	101%	99%
	(8)	(23)

THE ELECTORAL STAKES AND THE ELECTORAL-ECONOMIC CYCLE

Elections differ in how much is at stake. An election year in which an incumbent president seeks re-election is far more important, from the perspective of the incumbent administration, than a midterm congressional election. The incentives for producing a booming pre-election economy are greater in some election years than in others. Is it true, then, that the greater the electoral stakes, the greater the likelihood and the greater the magnitude of pre-election economic acceleration?

The short-run stimulation of the economy for electoral purposes involves several possible costs to an administration: inflationary pressures, destabilization, political attacks on deficit spending or the other policy instruments used to stimulate the economy, disruption of governmental programs due to shifts in the rate of government spending, political attacks on the fact of the stimulation itself, and having to forego stimulation at other times when it might be useful for long-run economic management. Such costs are more tolerable, of course, when the potential electoral benefits are greater.

From the vantage point of the incumbent administration—particularly the incumbent president—years can be ordered from maximum to minimum electoral importance:

1. On-years, incumbent president seeking re-election
2. Midterm congressional elections
3. On-years, incumbent president not seeking re-election
4. Odd-numbered years

There are surely special incentives to the administration in those on-years when the incumbent president seeks re-election; his direct personal interest in political survival coincides with what must be a particularly tempting opportunity to hit the economic accelerator. In those on-years when the incumbent president is not seeking re-election, his interest is not so clear. While his political party would inevitably consider more important all on-year over all off-year elections, a president might quite reasonably consider the congressional elections in the middle of his term as more important than an election at the conclusion of his political career. Success at midterm—or at least curbing the losses of his congressional allies, which is about the best the president can expect in an off-year—may allow him to maintain the force and continuity of his program, and may also serve as the beginnings of a drive for re-election. The downgrading of the

23

electoral importance (from the president's point of view) of the on-year when he is retiring is reinforced by the apparent ambivalence that presidents seem to have felt toward their party's nomination of a successor (consider Truman-Stevenson in 1952, Eisenhower-Nixon in 1960, and Johnson-Humphrey in 1968—the only relevant cases in many years). Finally on our list, there is no doubt that odd-numbered years are the least important electorally.

Having ranked the electoral importance of each year of a president's term, we can test the prediction that the greater the political importance of the year, the greater the efforts that an administration will make to accelerate the economy. Table 1-3 shows the clear link between the extent of economic well-being and the electoral importance of the year: *the greater the electoral stakes, the greater the economic improvement.* Real disposable income increased an average of 3.4 percent in years when the incumbent president sought re-election, 2.6 percent in midterm election years, 2.0 percent in those on-years when the incumbent president did not seek re-election, and a dismal 1.5 percent in odd-numbered years.[25]

The most important finding here—the difference between presidential elections when an incumbent seeks re-election and other years—holds over the entire set of elections from 1946 to 1976, *including* the Eisenhower years. During those thirty-one years, the median rate of growth in real disposable income per capita was

3.3 percent in years when the incumbent president sought re-election

compared to

1.7 percent in all other years.

[25] Let E_i = real disposable income per capita in year i. The annual change (in percentage terms) in real disposable income per capita is simply

$$\Delta E = \frac{E_i - E_{i-1}}{E_{i-1}} \times 100.$$

In Chapter 5, ΔE will be related to the national vote for members of the incumbent (White House) party.

TABLE 1-3

ANNUAL CHANGE IN REAL DISPOSABLE INCOME PER CAPITA
IN RELATION TO THE POLITICAL COMPLEXION OF THE YEARS,
ALL POSTWAR ADMINISTRATIONS EXCEPT EISENHOWER'S

	No election	On-year, incumbent president not seeking re-election	Midterm election	On-year, incumbent president seeking re-election
1946			−2.6%	
1947	−5.9%			
1948				3.4%
1949	−1.5%			
1950			5.9%	
1951	0.9%			
1952		1.1%		
1961	1.0%			
1962			2.6%	
1963	1.9%			
1964				5.6%
1965	4.8%			
1966			3.9%	
1967	3.0%			
1968		2.8%		
1969	1.5%			
1970			3.0%	
1971	2.6%			
1972				3.3%
1973	5.9%			
1974			−2.3%	
1975	1.0%			
1976				3.3%
Median amount	1.5%	2.0%	2.8%	3.4%

The rhetoric of policy initiatives matches the reality of the electoral-economic cycle. A content analysis of presidential State of the Union messages from 1946 to 1969 revealed that the most important topic after international relations was social welfare and allocative policy, and that its importance varied with the presidential election cycle and the term of the president:

> . . . the modal activity in this policy area is for the president to respond to the claim of a single segment of American society by asking Congress to pass legislation to confer some benefit on them.

The temporal pattern in this policy area is almost the opposite to that characteristic of international involvement. The distribution of social benefits is primarily a first term phenomenon. It rises gradually, but does not overshadow the more important international policy area until the president's fourth year in office. When faced with re-election needs, he is likely to be bountiful. But during a president's second term, the loadings on this factor fall sharply.

One might argue that a second term president does not have much influence with Congress and hence is less likely to urge them to undertake new activities. Whether or no, it does seem clear that there are political gains accruing from giving population groupings benefits they want: health, welfare assistance, housing, consumer protection, and so forth. Presidents attempt to distribute this largess when they have the greatest need to increase their political support.[26]

CONCLUSION

There is, then, an electoral rhythm to the national economic performance of many capitalist democracies. The

26 John H. Kessel, "The Parameters of Presidential Politics," *Social Science Quarterly* (June 1974), 8-24, at pp. 11-14.

electoral cycle causes substantial macroeconomic fluctuations.

In the United States, the electoral-economic cycle from 1948 to 1976 (other than the Eisenhower years) has consisted of:

—A two-year cycle in the growth of real disposable income per capita, with accelerations in even-numbered years and decelerations in odd-numbered years.

—A four-year presidential cycle in the unemployment rate, with downturns in unemployment in the months before the presidential election and upturns in the unemployment rate usually beginning from twelve to eighteen months after the election.

These patterns are consistent with the character of the economic tools available to control real disposable income and unemployment. Real disposable income—which is directly and immediately affected by taxes and transfer payments—can be manipulated in the short run. The unemployment rate, by contrast, is affected by fiscal and monetary policies that act more slowly and with more uncertain time lags on unemployment than do taxes and transfers on real disposable income.

Further, the greater the electoral stakes, the greater the economic stimulation. In particular, those years when incumbent presidents sought re-election enjoyed the most favorable short-run economic conditions. It comes as no surprise, however, to discover that upon re-election several of those incumbent presidents had to undertake, as their first economic priority, deflationary policies.

Like a detective in a murder mystery, I have tried so far to establish a motive and to find a pattern. The questions that remain are those of means and opportunity: How is the electoral-economic cycle produced? What specific instruments of economic policy are involved?

2

The Electoral Cycle and Economic Policy

Production of the electoral-economic cycle originates with a theory of elections held by politicians and their economic advisers, who believe that the electorate rewards short-run prosperity and punishes recession. Here I shall describe some of the instruments of economic policy that have translated the politicians' theory into the reality of election-year accelerations in real disposable income and possible reductions in the unemployment rate.

What are the economic policies used to stimulate the economy, or at least to reward certain groups of voters, in the months before the election? Conversely, what are the political constraints on economic policy options in election years? What is the incidence of economic benefits and costs attending election-year economic stimulation? An understanding of the redistributional effects of electoral economics deserves attention not only on its own but also because it may help explain the historical correlation between election-year prosperity and electoral support for incumbents.

In seeking to link economic policies to the timing of elections, we should keep in mind that just because something happens in an election year does not always mean that the fact of the election inspired the economic policy. No doubt certain economic policies are innocent of political interests and are entirely justified by technical macroeconomic considerations that would be compelling to incumbent and non-incumbent politicians alike if they understood them. In addition, the politicians' ideology and conception of what is best for the general welfare—rather than short-run electoral calculations—determine many policy choices, whether wisely or not.

28

Further, it is obvious, though no less important for being obvious, that powerful factors not related to elections determine the path of national economies. Non-political determinants of economic policy and performance may often completely dominate short-run efforts at pre-election economic tinkering. It is equally important to be realistic about the ability of politicians and their economic advisers to influence the course of a large national economy systematically and to do so with precise timing.

TRANSFER PAYMENTS AND THE ELECTORAL CYCLE

The key economic element in the electoral-economic cycle is real disposable income. The quickest way to produce an acceleration in real disposable income is for the government to mail more people larger checks—that is, for transfer payments to increase.

At the end of 1976 federal government transfers in the United States reached an annual rate of nearly $200 billion. About half of the total transfers were OASDHI payments—old age, survivors, disability, and health insurance benefits.[1]

Social security payments are the largest part of OASDHI transfers. As of 1976, these payments consisted of monthly checks mailed to 32 million citizens. After enactment of the Social Security Acts of 1935 and 1939, Congress legislated and the president signed a series of laws increasing benefits, with the first major increase in September 1950; increases followed in September 1952, September 1954, January 1959, January 1965, February 1968, January 1970, January 1971, September 1972, March-May 1974, June 1974, June 1975, and June 1976.[2] Nine of the 13 increases

[1] *Annual Report of the Council of Economic Advisers* (Washington, D.C.: U.S. Government Printing Office, 1977), p. 211.

[2] Benefit increases following 1974 were tied to a cost-of-living indicator. This indexing of social security lead to automatic increases of 8 percent in June 1975 and 6.4 percent in June 1976. The data reported here are from various monthly issues of the *Social Security Bulletin* (U.S. Department of Health, Education, and Welfare) and from the *Social Security Bulletin: Annual Statistical Supplement,*

took place in even-numbered years, generating a median election-year increase of 13 percent compared to 8 percent in odd-numbered years (Table 2-1). In addition, a more subtle sign of the electoral-economic cycle emerges from the historical record once we notice that benefits increased either at the beginning of the calendar year in January or at some time within the year. Comparing within-year increases with beginning-of-year increases in relation to elections reveals the following relationship for the 13 benefit increases:

	Within-year increase	Beginning-of-year increase
Election year	8	1
Odd-numbered year	1	3

Thus all but one of the within-year increases took place in an election year, usually in a scramble a few months before the election (Table 2-1). It is as if politicians believed that voters would not remember increased payments more than a few months. To insure that no beneficiary missed the point, every newly increased social security check since 1954 has been accompanied by a notice containing the name of the incumbent president.[3] In October 1972, for example, the check,

---

1973 and 1974. The legislative history of social security in relation to election years is described by John F. Manley, *The Politics of Finance* (Boston: Little, Brown, 1971), pp. 277-280.

[3] The administration made several other large-scale mailings to beneficiaries of transfer payments in 1972. The Department of Agriculture, the Department of Labor, the Office of Economic Opportunity, and the Veterans Administration sent out some 40 million brochures with pictures and quotations of President Nixon. Copies of the brochures, their costs, lists of recipients, and the White House actions leading to their production are found in the published volumes of the Ervin Committee: Executive Session Hearings before the Senate Select Committee on Presidential Campaign Activities, *Presidential Campaign Activities of 1972, Watergate and Related Activities: Use of Incumbency—Responsiveness Program* (Washington, D.C.: U.S. Government Printing Office, 1974), book 19, pp. 9135-9305. Books 18 and 19 of these hearings significantly contribute to the literature of political campaigning and show the diverse ways in which an incumbent president can target the economic and other resources of the government to promote his re-election.

increased by 20 percent, came along with a note (Figure 2-1) that the increase was due to a new law "enacted by the Congress and signed into law by President Richard Nixon."[4]

TABLE 2-1

EFFECTIVE DATE OF BENEFIT INCREASES IN SOCIAL SECURITY

Within-year increase		Beginning-of-year increase	
Date	% increase	Date	% increase
September 1950	About 77% over	January 1959	7%
	benefits in 1939 Act	January 1965	7%
September 1952	12.5%	January 1970	15%
September 1954	13%	January 1971	10%
February 1968	13%		
September 1972	20%		
March-May 1974	7%		
June 1974	4%		
June 1975*	8%		
June 1976*	6.4%		

* Increases of June 1975 and June 1976 resulted from new provisions (of 1972 Social Security Act) for automatic cost-of-living increases.

The pre-election increase in benefits tells only half the story, since the new benefits must be financed by increases in payroll taxes paid by the working population. Such increases in tax contributions start up only at the beginning of the calendar year, in part because of the difficulties in administering a within-year increase in the total taxable income base for social security. As a result, within-year increases in benefits are not matched by increases in the payroll tax until the start

[4] Charles Colson, a White House aide, wrote on a memorandum sent to him describing the various brochure mailings that on the "next notice re: 20% increase—RN wants to review personally" (Malek Exhibit No. 29, *Presidential Campaign Activities of 1972*, Book 18, p. 8427).

Higher social security payments

Your social security payment has been increased by 20 percent, starting with this month's check, by a new statute enacted by the Congress and signed into law by President Richard Nixon on July 1, 1972.

The President also signed into law a provision which will allow your social security benefits to increase automatically if the cost of living goes up. Automatic benefit increases will be added to your check in future years according to the conditions set out in that law.

U.S. Department of
Health, Education, and Welfare
Social Security Administration
DHEW Publication No. (SSA) 73-10322
October 1972

FIGURE 2-1

LETTER OF OCTOBER 1972 TO 24,760,000 SOCIAL SECURITY BENEFICIARIES

of the following year, after the election. All this leads to an increase in real disposable income before the election among those receiving social security benefits that is financed after the election by those paying the payroll tax. Figure 2-2 shows the gap in the flow of checks from and to the government, the pre-election pay-out and the post-election pay-in, for the period around the 1972 presidential election. This election-time gap resembles the "window in space" for launching a space rocket; there is a short period of good feeling (toward incumbents) when pre-election economic extravagances have not yet been burnt up by their post-election costs.[5] Since the units of measurement in Figure 2-2 are

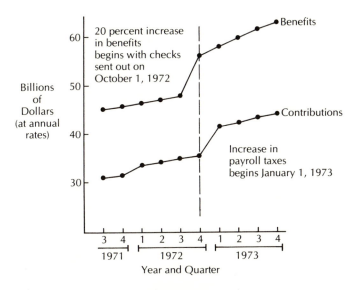

FIGURE 2-2

PRE-ELECTION PAY-OUT OF BENEFITS AND POST-ELECTION
PAY-IN OF CONTRIBUTIONS

[5] The analogy was used by an anonymous British politician to characterize the proper time for the government to call an election; see David Butler and Michael Pinto-Duschinsky, *The British General*

tens of billions of dollars, this is hardly a trivial matter. Congress partially shut down this game after the over-exuberance of 1972 by indexing benefit increases to the inflation rate, with the increase taking place each June. As we shall see, it was not the only game in town.

Consistent with the pattern of displacing costs until after elections, the growth in what the government misleadingly calls "contributions for social insurance"—the federal payroll tax for social security and unemployment insurance—has tended to increase more rapidly in odd-numbered years than in election years. From 1946 to 1975, these taxes have moved with the electoral cycle (greater growth in odd-numbered years than in the surrounding election years) in 17 years and shifted contrary to the cycle in 11 years, with one year a tie. Particularly sharp increases have followed recent presidential elections. Payroll taxes increased by $4.1 billion in 1968 but by $6.2 billion in 1969, exceeding the long-run upward trend. In 1972 the increase was $7.9 billion, but in 1973 it shot up to $16.6 billion for a total contribution of $79.4 billion.

The payroll tax is collected as a fixed proportion of an individual's income during the course of the year, beginning in January, until a legislated income ceiling is reached. For example, in 1972 the payroll tax was assessed on the first $9,000 earned during the course of a calendar year, and in 1976 on the first $15,300. These arrangements have introduced substantial seasonality into the tax take because people earning more than ceiling complete their total yearly contribution relatively early in the year. This seasonality in payments peps up the economy late in the year around election time, aggravating "the already inherent tendency of the economy to . . . soar in the fall."[6]

Election of 1970 (London: Macmillan, 1971), pp. 349-350. The "magic window" also describes the jiggling of budget calendars "so that there is an overlap, or 'window,' that accelerates extra aid into the short run at no apparent extra cost" (Francis X. Clines, "About New York," *New York Times*, March 19, 1977, p. 17).

[6] John A. Brittain, *The Payroll Tax for Social Security* (Washington, D.C.: The Brookings Institution, 1972), p. 237.

Further, the mechanism for collecting the payroll tax gives those earning more than the maximum taxable amount an increase in real income in the later part of the year, after they have completed their total yearly contribution. In 1972, for example, the real disposable income of those earning over $13,000 in salary increased in September. And obviously the greater the income, the earlier in the year (and farther from election time) the total payment is completed.

No supportable claim can be made that the timing of the payroll tax increases forms part of a systematic fiscal policy designed to keep the economy on an even keel. On the contrary, "increases in the payroll tax structure appear to have contributed significantly to the intensity of recessions when imposed during the slack period of the 1930s, and before and during three recessions after World War II."[7]

Social security increases require the joint action of the Congress and the president. In such election years as 1972, with a Republican president and a Democratic Congress, it seems reasonable to expect a bidding process growing from efforts to obtain the political credit for a generous improvement in social security benefits. In late 1971, President Nixon proposed a 5 percent increase for 1972, which was eventually trumped by the Democratic Congress that increased benefits by 20 percent. The bidding sequence went as follows:

PRE-CAMPAIGN (LATE 1971)
—5 percent increase passed by House, "guided through by Wilbur Mills"
—5 percent increase for 1972 advocated by President Nixon

PRIMARY CAMPAIGN (EARLY 1972)
—15 percent increase proposed by Muskie (before New Hampshire primary)
—20 percent increase proposed by Mills (before New Hampshire, when Mills was a candidate in the presidential primaries)

[7] Ibid.

35

—20 percent increase then proposed by Muskie (still before New Hampshire)

—25 percent increase proposed by Humphrey (after New Hampshire, before Wisconsin)

PRESIDENTIAL CAMPAIGN

—20 percent increase passed by House and Senate, July 1, 1972, despite hints of presidential veto

—20 percent increase effective September 1, 1972, signed into law by President Nixon

—20 percent increase in social security checks sent out on October 1, 1972.[8]

As a result, $8.0 billion of the $15.2 billion rise in personal income in October 1972—the month immediately preceding the presidential election—was accounted for by the rise in social security benefits.

VETERANS BENEFITS

Payments to veterans represent the second largest component (after OASDHI payments) in government transfers. From 1945 to 1976, the government paid $250 billion in veterans benefits. In 1976, $19.0 billion was distributed among 29 million veterans, their 66 million dependents, and 4 million relatives of deceased veterans.[9] It is hard to imagine how so much money could flow to so many people without some political channeling.

Legislation enacted by Congress and signed by the president has in fact produced significant pre-election increases in the stream of veterans benefits. Figure 2-3, showing the quarterly changes in paid benefits, makes clear the local

[8] This sequence of events was recorded in the *New York Times* on the following dates in 1972: February 24, p. 19; February 27, p. IV-12; February 29, p. 13; March 4, p. 12; March 12, p. III-4; March 29, p. 24; June 25, p. 33; July 1, p. 1; July 2, p. IV-2; October 3, p. 34; and October 4, p. 46.

[9] U.S. Bureau of the Census, *Statistical Abstract of the United States: 1976* (Washington, D.C.: U.S. Government Printing Office, 1976), pp. 326, 345-350.

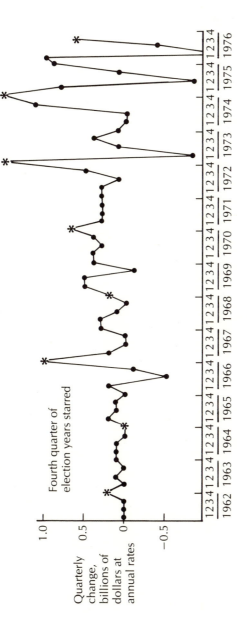

FIGURE 2-3

QUARTERLY CHANGES IN VETERANS BENEFITS

maxima achieved during the fourth quarter of election years. These surges are not simply a matter of payment of fall-term education benefits to veterans, because increases of this magnitude do not occur in the fall of years without elections. Since 1962, benefits have increased an average of $660 million (at annual rates) between the third and fourth quarters of election years, but only $220 million in years without elections. That election-year increase between the third and fourth quarters has, furthermore, exceeded the comparable increase in the odd-numbered year following the election in 5 of 6 elections (counting the one tie, the score becomes 5½ out of 7).

These findings, which replicate our results for social security payments, fit well with the model that led us to look at transfer payments in relation to elections: a sure way to increase the real disposable income of voters in election years is to mail them larger checks. Perhaps all this is a sign of the "liberal hour" described by Adlai Stevenson, that "moment just before presidential elections when even the most obsolete men become reconciled, if briefly and expediently," to the role of modern government in contributing to social and economic welfare.[10] It is true, at any rate, that greater national

[10] John Kenneth Galbraith, *The Liberal Hour* (Boston: Houghton Mifflin, 1960), p. vii. For good evidence, see John H. Kessel, "The Parameters of Presidential Politics," *Social Science Quarterly* (June 1974), 8-24.

Franklin D. Roosevelt in a campaign speech on October 23, 1940, struck a similar note with elegant political style:

> The tears, the crocodile tears, tears for the laboring man and laboring woman, now being shed in this campaign come from those same Republican leaders who had their chance to prove their love for labor in 1932—and missed it. . . .
> Back in 1932, they raised their hands in horror at the thought of fixing a minimum wage or maximum hours for labor; they never gave one thought to such things as pensions for old age or insurance for the unemployed.
> And in 1940, eight years later, what a different tune is played by them: It is a tune played against a sounding board of election day. It is a tune with overtones which whisper: "Votes, votes, votes, votes."

commitments to social welfare are made in election years than in years without elections.

ELECTIONS AND THE FLOW OF TRANSFER PAYMENTS

Governmental transfer payments—including social security, disability insurance, medicare, and other beneficiary payments—typically increase from month to month, in part simply reflecting a growing population and a larger pool of eligible beneficiaries. Normally, therefore, transfers reach their yearly maximum in December—at least in odd-numbered years (Figure 2-4). *But in four of the last seven election years, governmental transfer payments have reached their yearly peak in October or November; in the eight surrounding odd-numbered years, in contrast, transfers reached their yearly maximum at the end of the year in December (with one exception).* Figure 2-5 shows the autumnal heaping of transfer payments for the election years of 1962, 1964, 1970, and 1972. The heaping—or, as it may be referred to technically, *biennial kyphosis*, after the Greek *kyphos* for "heap" or "hump"[11]—probably occurs because those government agencies sending out checks are able, with the stimulation of an election year, to accelerate processing of new beneficiary applications, the payment of retroactive benefits, and the initiation of new programs. Perhaps some agencies are simply more responsive to the needs of both their clients and their political patrons under the lash of an election. Others may be prodded by the staff of a powerful president

---

This tune is, of course, only a rehash of the tune of 1936, a little louder. In that election year the affection of these Republican leaders for the laboring man also rose to a high pitch. But after election day. . . .

[11] Kyphotic phenomena are discussed in the statistical literature under the name of data "heaping" requiring pre-analysis smoothing. For citations to other examples and discussion see Richard Hobson, "Properties Preserved by Some Smoothing Functions," *Journal of the American Statistical Association*, 71 (September 1976), 763-766.

39

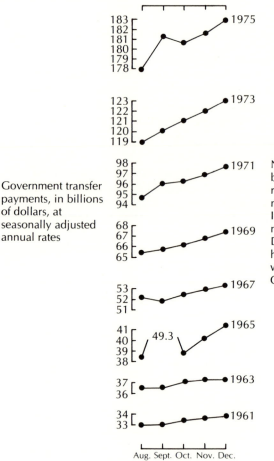

Government transfer payments, in billions of dollars, at seasonally adjusted annual rates

Note steady month-by-month increase, reaching yearly maximum in December. In all 8 odd-numbered years, December's transfers have exceeded November's, which have exceeded October's.

FIGURE 2-4

THE PATH OF TRANSFER PAYMENTS IN THE FALL OF ODD-NUMBERED YEARS

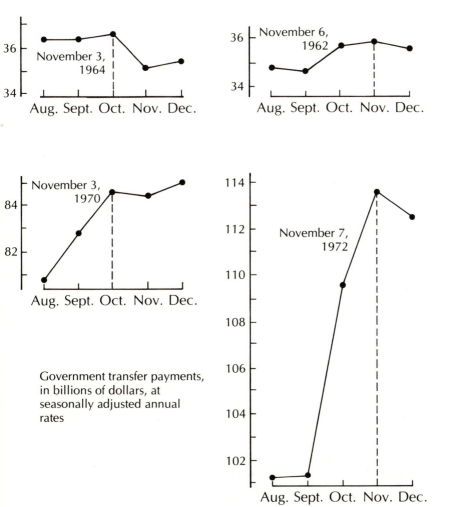

FIGURE 2-5
HEAPING OF TRANSFER PAYMENTS IN 1962, 1964, 1970,
AND 1972; VARIETIES OF KYPHOSIS IN RELATION
TO THE DATE OF THE ELECTION

to catch up completely on back claims before the election. Thus some of the business normally done in Decembers (in odd-numbered years at least) gets done in October and November of election years. It is, in the language of governmental spending, accelerated procurement.

One puzzle is why election-year transfers, recorded here on a cash-delivered basis, should sometimes peak in even-numbered Novembers (biennial novemkyphosis) rather than in Octobers (octokyphosis). Since elections are held on the first Tuesday in November, does not a November heaping of transfer payments come too late? Let us consider one speculative answer. The key date is always November 3, for it is on that day (weekends excepted) that October's beneficiary payments are actually delivered in the mail boxes. The checks are sent to post offices before the third of the month with instructions from the Treasury to deliver the checks on the third (see Figure 2-6). Now if the election in a particular year is "late"—that is, if the first Tuesday in November falls on the sixth or the seventh—then a November heaping of

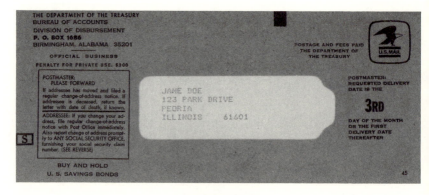

FIGURE 2-6
DELIVERY INSTRUCTIONS ON THE SOCIAL SECURITY
ENVELOPE

transfers will still get there in time. If the election falls earlier in November, then November's transfers will not reach the voters before the election. This sequencing suggests a cynical prediction: octokyphosis will occur when the election is early, novemkyphosis will occur if there is a late election date. As Figure 2-5 shows, such is the case for the four elections in which heaping occurred. In two elections taking place on the third, an October heaping came to pass; in elections on the sixth and the seventh, a November heaping. Of those years—1962, 1964, 1970, and 1972—it may be said that not a trick was missed.

Why does kyphosis, of either variety, arise in some election years and not in others? What are 1962, 1964, 1970, and 1972 trying to tell us? What happened, or rather failed to happen, in those akyphotic years of 1966, 1968, 1974, and 1976?

Kyphosis reflects the president's ability to mobilize the bureaucracy and the Congress to give real disposable income an extra stimulative kick via transfer payments right before the election. Kyphosis is a sign of presidential power. When the president is strong, kyphosis should be more likely to appear. The presidency was in fact strong in 1962, 1964, 1970, and 1972, indeed much stronger than it was in 1966, 1968, 1974, and 1976. In the four kyphotic election years, for example, the president's approval ratings in the January Gallup poll were 78 percent, 80 percent, 62 percent, and 49 percent (and rising). In the akyphotic election years, the ratings were 61 percent (but falling), 47 percent, 27 percent, and 46 percent.[12] Biennial kyphosis in transfer payments may not result so much from direct White House intervention into

[12] Data are from *The Gallup Opinion Index*, 125 (November-December 1975), 17-24. Mayhew makes a similar argument with regard to the president's influence over members of Congress: "Of course when the president's poll ratings drop, so do his ability to punish and reward and his influence over congressmen. When they drop very low, it becomes politically profitable for congressman of his own party to attack him—as with Democrats in 1951-52 and Republicans in 1973-74" (David R. Mayhew, *Congress: The Electoral Connection* [New Haven: Yale University Press, 1974], p. 43, n. 67).

the administration of transfer payments as from the desire of those agencies administering transfers to stay out of trouble with a powerful incumbent and to avoid election-year criticism of delays in mailing checks to the elderly, the infirm, and the poor.

Octokyphosis may be the wave of the future, given the change of dates in the federal government's fiscal year. Until 1977, the fiscal year ran from July 1 to June 30. In order to help smooth the congressional process for considering the federal budget, fiscal years have been changed to run from October 1 to September 30. Thus FY78 began October 1, 1977. The change in dates makes a twofold contribution to pre-election economic acceleration. First, increases in spending start up at the beginning of the new fiscal year (for example, the federal pay raise began on October 1, 1977). Presumably increases in transfer payments will also become synchronized to the October schedule. Second, there is the modest uptick in government spending at the very end of the fiscal year, now only six weeks from election day, as agencies seek to exhaust their yearly spending allotment (the "use it or lose it" principle).[13]

In summary, the evidence describes the key role of transfer payments in producing election-year economic stimulation. The mechanisms at work include pre-election increases in the level of transfer payments, the creation of an electoral-economic "window" by deferring the costs of pre-election increases in transfers until after the election, and administrative fiddling with the timing of autumn transfers (kyphosis) in election years. All three of these devices operated in the 1972 Nixon re-election campaign and they operated at a more intense level, involving more money, than in any other election.

---

[13] Executive officials use broad discretion in determining the timing of spending. See Louis Fisher, *Presidential Spending Power* (Princeton: Princeton University Press, 1975), chapter 6. On President Carter's order against a late September spending spree at the end of the transition quarter going into FY78, see Linda Charlton, "Should Old Allotments Be Forgot at the End of Federal Fiscal Year?" *New York Times*, October 1, 1977, p. 25.

ECONOMIC POLICY AND PERFORMANCE DURING THE 1972
PRESIDENTIAL CAMPAIGN

In accounting for Republican losses in the 1954 and 1958
congressional elections as well as his own loss in the 1960
presidential election, Richard Nixon stressed the importance
of pre-election economic downturns in the two or three
months immediately preceding the election. His presidential
re-election campaign of 1972, though, enjoyed a booming
economy, with a particularly sharp upturn in the fall. Figure
2-7 shows the quarterly path of real disposable income per
capita during 1971-1973, with its ever-accelerating climb to
the fourth quarter of 1972 followed by post-election decay.
The exquisite political precision of this economic course
must have been partly the result of sheer good luck for the
incumbents. Much of the pre-election economic acceleration
was, however, the result of deliberate planning and the mo-
bilization of policy instruments producing acceleration in real
disposable income growth. Let us look for motives, means,
and opportunities in pre-election economic policy in 1971-
1972.[14]

Three of the men in government most directly controlling
economic policy before the 1972 election—Richard Nixon,
Arthur Burns, and Herbert Stein—all firmly believed in the
theory that the electorate rewards incumbents for an improving pre-election economy. Herbert Stein had written a detailed history of U.S. fiscal policy in which one of the major
explanatory variables used to account for policy choices was

[14] Economic histories of the period include Hearings before the
Joint Economic Committee, *The 1973 Midyear Review of the
Economy* (Washington, D.C.: U.S. Government Printing Office,
1974); Rodney J. Morrison, *Expectations and Inflation: Nixon,
Politics, and Economics* (Lexington, Massachusetts: Lexington Books,
1973); Herbert Stein, "Fiscal Policy: Reflections on the Past
Decade," in *Contemporary Economic Problems*, ed. William Fellner
(Washington, D.C.: American Enterprise Institute, 1976), pp. 55-84;
and Leonard Silk, *Nixonomics*, 2nd ed. (New York: Praeger, 1973).

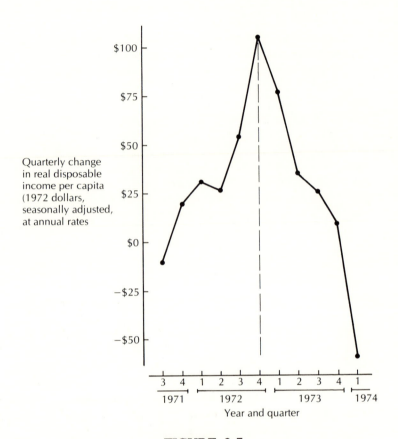

FIGURE 2-7
QUARTERLY CHANGES IN REAL DISPOSABLE INCOME
SURROUNDING THE 1972 ELECTION

whether the year was an election year or not;[15] Nixon had blamed his past electoral defeats on poor pre-election economic performance; and Burns had proposed to Nixon that the economy be stimulated in the months before the 1960 election. Nixon recounted the 1960 episode in his *Six Crises*:

> Early in March, Dr. Arthur F. Burns, the former chairman of the President's Council of Economic Advisers and probably the nation's top authority on the economic cycle, called on me in my office in the Capitol . . . he expressed great concern about the way the economy was then acting . . . Burns' conclusion was that unless some decisive governmental action were taken, and taken soon, we were heading for another economic dip which would hit its low point in October, just before the elections. He urged strongly that everything possible be done to avert this development. He urgently recommended that two steps be

[15] Herbert Stein, *The Fiscal Revolution in America* (Chicago: University of Chicago Press, 1969). Later, as a policy-maker himself, Stein wrote a spoofing but perceptive description of the wage-price freeze and the "Nixon shocks" of August 1971 (quoted in William Safire, *Before the Fall* [Garden City, N.Y.: Doubleday, 1975], pp. 522-523):

> On the 15th day of the 8th month the President came down from the mountain and spoke to the people on all networks, saying:
> I bring you a Comprehensive Eight-point Program, as follows:
> First, thou shall raise no price, neither any wage, rent, interest, fee or dividend.
> Second, thou shall pay out no gold, neither metallic nor paper. . . .
> Seventh, thou shall enjoy in 1972 what the Democrats promised thee for 1973.

In the summer of 1971 pollster Albert Sindlinger met with White House Nixon aides Colson and Haldeman and reported that Nixon was in trouble with the electorate over economic conditions, particularly inflation. Wheeler reports that "according to Colson, the decision to impose the wage-price freeze was based largely on polls which showed that it was essential that the president take forceful action to bring inflation under control." The episode is described in Michael Wheeler, *Lies, Damn Lies, and Statistics: The Manipulation of Public Opinion in America* (New York: Liveright, 1976), pp. 11-12.

taken immediately: by loosening up on credit and, where justifiable, by increasing spending for national security. The next time I saw the President, I discussed Burns' proposals with him, and he in turn put the subject on the agenda for the next Cabinet meeting.

The matter was thoroughly discussed by the Cabinet but, for two reasons, Burns' recommendation that immediate action be taken along the lines he had suggested did not prevail. First, several of the Administration's economic experts who attended the meeting did not share his bearish prognosis of the economic prospects. Second, even assuming his predictions might be right, there was strong sentiment against using the spending and credit powers of the Federal Government to affect the economy, unless and until conditions clearly indicated a major recession in prospect.

In supporting Burns' point of view, I must admit that I was more sensitive politically than some of the others around the cabinet table.[16]

There were, then, some hints from past history that the Nixon administration would seek to prepare the economy for the 1972 election. And within the government the point became clear; as one high-level economic official during that period put it later, "The word went out that 1972, by God, was going to be a good year." The 1971 economic forecasts predicted that the unemployment rate during 1972 would be 6 percent. This was unacceptable to the White House, and pre-election stimulus was sought. According to Sherman Maisel, a governor of the Federal Reserve from 1965 to 1972:

It was . . . clear to the White House where new expansionary pressures ought to be generated. The finger pointed

[16] Richard M. Nixon, *Six Crises* (Garden City, New York: Doubleday, 1962), pp. 309-310. A useful analysis of President Nixon's economic approach is found in Leonard Silk, "Tapes' Insight on Nixon: They Indicate His Economic Thinking Is Heavily Weighted by Political Factors," *New York Times*, August 7, 1974, p. 42.

right at the Federal Reserve. Because of the independent position of the Fed, no direct orders could be issued, but the White House made its views plain.

The rule of gradualism no longer satisfied George Shultz, director of the Office of Management and Budget and the strongest economic voice in the Administration. He now espoused an activist monetary policy. Money would determine spending. If an election were to be won, the Federal Reserve would have to increase the money supply at far more than the 4.2 percent average of 1969-70. In his words, the "real juice" for the expanding economy had to come from monetary policy. To make the message clear, the statement in OMB's official briefing chart book that called attention to the need for an adequate money supply growth was printed in bright red. The estimates of how fast money was to grow were not as precise, but in various speeches and off-the-record briefings, the range of 6 to 9 percent became clear.[17]

The Fed accelerated the growth of money in 1971-1972. Whether it did so because of the election or for some other reason remains a matter of controversy.[18] Critics of the Fed

[17] Sherman J. Maisel, *Managing the Dollar* (New York: Norton, 1973), pp. 267-268. This quotation (as well as my analysis of 1972) takes us into the difficult area of attributing motivation to particular policy actions that can often be justified on many grounds. George P. Shultz, in response to Maisel's analysis, points out that the Democratic critics of the administration sought greater economic stimulus in 1972 and, furthermore, "Through all of this, I find it hard to disentangle objective economic advice designed to produce a healthy economy from politically motivated actions. Certainly, I know that I did not try to produce an economy stimulated in an unhealthy way. In that spirit, I cannot accept the implication of the Maisel statement, 'If the election were to be won, . . .' " (Letter of December 27, 1976, to Edward R. Tufte.)

[18] Charges of the political responsiveness of the Fed in the 1972 campaign are found in Paul Lewis, "Facing Up to Arthur Burns," *New York Times*, July 11, 1976, section 5, p. 5; Maisel, *Managing the Dollar*; Sanford Rose, "The Agony of the Federal Reserve," *Fortune*, 90 (July 1974), 90-93, 180-190; Paul Lewis, "Challenging the Olympian Fed," *New York Times*, August 18, 1974, section 3, p. 1; and Jack Anderson, "Politics and the Economy," *New York Post*,

have pointed to Burns's ties with Nixon for many years and the Burns-Nixon proposal to stimulate the economy before the 1960 election. Its defenders have given character references for Burns and have sought to justify the expansionary policy on economic grounds.[19] What is probably more important is that the 1972 election was nothing special. Historically the supply of money has increased more rapidly in the two years before presidential elections than in the two years following. Table 2-2 totes up changes in the biennial growth rate in money stock (M_1, currency plus demand deposits) in relation to presidential elections.[20] The relationship is a

---

March 12, 1975. William Safire's *Before the Fall*, in a chapter appropriately titled "Hardball," describes in detail the administration pressure on Burns in 1971-72.

[19] Arthur Burns wrote to Senator Proxmire about some of the issues: "Money Supply in the Conduct of Monetary Policy," *Federal Reserve Bulletin*, 59 (November 1973), 791-798; other defences are found in "Letters to Fortune," *Fortune*, 90 (August 1974), 113, and "Letters: Controversy Over Burns and Fed's Role," *New York Times*, September 1, 1974, section 3, p. 10. The whole sorry episode illustrates the problems of evidence in the attribution of political motivation to a *particular* economic policy in the short run. An interesting discussion of the policy choices of the Open Market Committee of the Federal Reserve System is found in Sandford F. Borins, "The Political Economy of 'The Fed,'" *Public Policy*, 20 (Spring 1972), 175-198, particularly pp. 196-198.

[20] The *biennial* rate of growth of M_1 is used because of the well-documented "long lags in the response of the real sectors of the economy to changes in monetary policy." James L. Pierce, "The Trade-Off Between Short- and Long-Term Policy Goals," reprinted in Warren L. Smith and Ronald L. Teigen, ed., *Readings in Money, National Income, and Stabilization Policy*, 3rd ed. (Homewood, Ill.: Richard D. Irwin, 1974), p. 370; see also Michael J. Hamburger, "The Impact of Monetary Variables," ibid., 376-390. Biennial growth rates are also reported in Jürg Niehans, "How to Fill an Empty Shell," *American Economic Review*, 66 (May 1976), 177-183. The measure M_1 combines demand deposits at commercial banks and currency in circulation. It turns out that demand deposits make up the bulk of M_1; in January 1975, for example, demand deposits were $221.3 billion and currency in circulation $73.7 billion. Since a great diversity of factors might affect ups and downs in demand deposits, Table 2 was recomputed for that part of the money supply most directly

strong one, especially when the Eisenhower years are excluded (as they should be). Most biennial changes in the growth of M_1 have assisted rather than retarded the electoral-economic cycle. It appears that anti-inflationary zeal flourishes in the politically slack period after presidential elections, rarely before.

TABLE 2-2

CHANGES IN MONEY STOCK, TWO-YEAR PERIODS, 1948-1976

| | Biennial periods | |
| | Prior to the presidential election | After the presidential election |
For 1948-1976		
Rate of growth of money supply increased	4	1
Rate of growth of money supply decreased	3	6

| | Biennial periods | |
| | Prior to the presidential election | After the presidential election |
For 1948-1976, except Eisenhower years		
Rate of growth of money supply increased	4	1
Rate of growth of money supply decreased	1	4

(The connection between movements in the money supply and the timing of elections has become especially important —and touchy—since 1971 because of the rapid growth in the currency assets of the major capitalist countries. Among

under the control of the government, the amount of currency printed and coin stamped (M_0?). The link between the biennial growth rate and elections remained. The currency data are recorded in the monthly *Federal Reserve Bulletin* and the Fed's *Supplement to Banking and Monetary Statistics.*

OECD nations currency assets increased nearly threefold from 1971 to 1976 thereby, among other things, enhancing the possibilities for election-year stimulation. I return to this point in Chapter 3.)

Although fiscal and monetary policy did their share in producing the 1972 acceleration in real disposable income growth, it was an autumn increase in transfer payments that produced the immediate pre-election economic surge. A 20 percent increase in October's social security checks (accompanied by the letter) financed by the post-election increase in contributions combined with novemkyphosis to put together a great increase in pre-election real disposable income. That is hardly the end of the story, however. Almost every type of transfer—not just social security—accelerated in late 1972 and decelerated after the election.[21] The payment of

[21] Transfers in the 1972 campaign were administered with high political spirit, and part of the flow of federal money came under the heavy-handed influence of the White House "Responsiveness Program." The aims and methods of that sleazy program have been captured in some 1,200 pages of memoranda put into the exhibits of the Senate Watergate (Ervin) Committee (cited in note 4 above). Although the documents must be heavily discounted for braggadocio, they do catalogue (much like Don Giovanni's Leporello) the range of policy instruments available for the pre-election targeting of government resources available, at least to those willing to go all out. After the election, in December 1972, the administration made heavy cuts in domestic spending, mainly through impoundment. On this, see Fisher, *Presidential Spending Power*, chapter 8. A Nixon White House aide acknowledged the role of electoral considerations in their economic policy:

> The mildly restrictive economic policies set in motion by the Republicans cooled the economy producing the mini-recession of 1970, which in turn prevented Republican political gains in the off-year. After that experience economics took a back seat to politics at the White House. Anxious not to enter a presidential year with the economy running at less than breakneck speed, the Republicans in 1971 and 1972 opened the sluices and the dollars flowed. Back-to-back $23 billion deficits were run in the two years preceding the election of 1972. To control the unpleasant side effects, such as a rising consumer price index, the GOP went down to the Democratic barn and stole the bridle of wage-and-price controls. Reviewing the election returns of November, 1972, the strategem

veterans benefits heaped up quite substantially toward the
end of 1972; the payments (in billions of dollars at annual
rates) for the twelve quarters from 1971 to 1973 were:

1971-1	10.8
-2	11.1
-3	11.4
-4	11.7
1972-1	12.0
-2	12.1
-3	12.6
-4	14.1 (election quarter)
1973-1	13.3
-2	13.4
-3	13.8
-4	13.9

Along with social security (or, more broadly, OASDHI
benefits) and veterans benefits, the other major source of direct government payments to voters consists of federal grants
in aid to state and local governments. The quarterly flow of
this money (in billions of dollars at annual rates) was im-
pressively kyphotic:

1971-1	27.1
-2	29.5
-3	29.8
-4	30.8
1972-1	32.2
-2	38.0
-3	34.4
-4	46.1 (that's right)
1973-1	41.1
-2	40.5
-3	40.5
-4	42.5

---

was not unsuccessful—politically. (Patrick J. Buchanan, *Conservative Votes, Liberal Victories* [New York: Quadrangle, 1975],
119-120.)

In 1972 many different kinds of transfer payments were accelerated for delivery before the election. Each little gimmick involved a relatively modest amount of money—but a billion here and a billion there, as the late Senator Dirksen once said, and pretty soon you're talking about real money. A good many citizens (perhaps 75 million), almost all of them of voting age, benefited directly from the increased cash flow from the government before the 1972 election. The increases in the amount of transfer payments came about because of legislation passed by Congress. Perhaps the best time for a liberal Congress to increase beneficiary payments in the face of a veto by a conservative president is during an election year, especially one in which the president is seeking re-election.[22] It appears that in 1972 President Nixon was willing to sacrifice conservative anti-spending principles and absorb ideological defeats on beneficiary legislation in exchange for the increased flow of transfers immediately before the election. In 1976, President Ford, one more loyal to conservative principles than Nixon, a loyalty enforced by the threat of Reagan on the right, was repeatedly placed in a politically awkward position by vetoes of spending legislation passed by a Democratic Congress. The frustration felt by Ford's supporters at his Eisenhower-like failure to tinker with an election-year economy was captured in this report of a news conference held by Ford's press secretary, Ronald Nessen:

> Mr. Nessen, testily rebutting speculation about electioneering with the mineral leasing bill, seemed to suggest that the best political defense was a bad offense. "To say that the President makes these kinds of decisions for political reasons is just to ignore a whole set of decisions the President has made this year which you yourselves have written about as being politically dumb," Mr. Nessen told reporters. He added: "If the President is interested only in

[22] Several examples are reported in Eileen Shanahan, "Washington Report: Much Unclear along the Potomac," *New York Times*, November 3, 1974, p. 3-15.

votes and only in delegates, why does he have the Pentagon draw up a list of bases to be closed? Why does he propose an energy program which is going to raise prices? Why does he propose an increase in Social Security taxes? Why does he hold New York City's feet to the fire and so forth? Why did he veto a tax cut on Christmas Eve, for goodness sake?"[23]

CONCLUSIONS: ECONOMIC POLICY AND THE ELECTORAL-ECONOMIC CYCLE

A major premise of modern economic stabilization policy is that macroeconomic fluctuations result from instabilities in market behavior—that is, the sources of fluctuations are internal to the economic system.[24] Or, if the sources are not internal, they are seen as being random and unsystematic. It appears from our evidence, however, that certain substantial macroeconomic fluctuations are simply the product of the routine rhythms of political life.[25]

[23] *New York Times*, July 3, 1976, p. 19. See also A. James Reichley, "Crossing the Ford Years," *Washington Post*, September 11, 1977, p. E4.

[24] Assar Lindbeck, "Stabilization Policy in Open Economies with Endogenous Politicians," *American Economic Review*, 66 (May 1976), 1-19. Lindbeck's paper is a subtle theoretical account of the timing of economic policy in relation to elections. Treating the actions of public authorities as exogenous leads to problems of estimation in macroeconomic models; see Stephen M. Goldfeld and Alan S. Blinder, "Some Implications of Endogenous Stabilization Policy," *Brookings Papers on Economic Activity*, 3 (1972), 585-644.

[25] Obviously other policies may revolve around the electoral (or the budget) cycle. U.S. policy toward Vietnam apparently was entangled with the timing of elections for two decades, as each administration was "caught in the same game. Rule 1 of that game is: 'Do not lose the rest of Vietnam to Communist control before the next election'" (Daniel Ellsberg, "The Quagmire Myth and the Stalemate Machine," *Public Policy*, 19 [Spring 1971], 217-274, at p. 252). Ellsberg quotes Kenneth O'Donnell's account ("LBJ and the Kennedys," *Life*, August 7, 1970) of a 1963 meeting between Senator Mansfield (who urged that the growing U.S. involvement be ended) and President Kennedy:

The electoral rhythm to national economic performance is pounded out (by those administrations that choose to do so) with several major instruments of economic control available to modern governments. The blunt but sure instrument—putting larger checks in the mail during the months before the election—is naturally favored in the short run. Stimulative policies with more uncertain lags—budgets deficits, increases in the supply of money—have also proved convenient to incumbents pursuing re-election. The electoral-economic cycle affects the flow of transfers to millions of citizens, and billions of dollars are involved.[26]

The United States has experienced two types of political-economic cycles: a two-year cycle of acceleration and deceleration in real disposable income, and a four-year pres-

---

The President told Mansfield that he had been having serious second thoughts about Mansfield's argument and that he now agreed with the Senator's thinking on the need for a complete military withdrawal from Vietnam.

"But I can't do that until 1965—after I'm reelected," Kennedy told Mansfield.

President Kennedy felt, and Mansfield agreed with him, that if he announced a total withdrawal of American military personnel from Vietnam before the 1964 election, there would be a wild conservative outcry against returning him to the Presidency for a second term.

After Mansfield left the office, the President told me that he had made up his mind that after his reelection he would take the risk of unpopularity and make a complete withdrawal of American forces from Vietnam. "In 1965, I'll be damned everywhere as a Communist appeaser. But I don't care. If I tried to pull out completely now, we would have another Joe McCarthy red scare on our hands, but I can do it after I'm reelected. So we had better make damned sure that I *am* reelected."

[26] There is very little comparative evidence available that bears on these points. Now that the key role of transfer payments in the electoral-economic cycle has been identified, it should be possible to investigate the instruments behind the cycle for many countries. See A. R. Prest, "Sense and Nonsense in Budgetary Policy," *Economic Journal*, 78 (March 1968), 5; and, in particular, Assar Lindbeck, "Fiscal Policy as a Tool of Economic Stabilization—Comments to an OECD Report," *Kyklos*, 23 (1970), 7-32.

idential cycle of high unemployment early in the term followed by economic stimulation, increasing prosperity, and reduced unemployment late in the term. The real income cycle is especially the product of election-year increases in transfer payments, administrative messing around with the timing of beneficiary payments, and decreases or postponements of taxes.[27] Thus election-year enhancement of real disposable income is significantly a political and a bureaucratic problem: legislation must be passed, room for discretionary spending found, and agency administrators energized. The successful maintenance of the two-year real income cycle does not require, nor does it demonstrate, any great skill at macroeconomic planning, management, or theory. It is not much more subtle than getting a lot of checks in the mail before the first Tuesday in November. In contrast, the four-year unemployment cycle may require some effective macroeconomic management, and perhaps this is one reason why the unemployment cycle is not as sharply defined as the two-year real income cycle.

The electorally salient characteristics of economic benefits (and patronage in general) are their timing and their location. As an important instrument behind the electoral-economic cycle, incumbents prefer increases in transfer payments not only because they more surely improve voters' economic well-being at the right time (compared to fiscal or monetary policies with their uncertain lags), but also because many types of transfer payments go to particular organized interests—veterans, the retired, those living in "impacted areas," and the like. Targeted benefits enable incumbents to tell all the members of that group what they did in particular for them. The effect is strengthened, of course, when the increased benefits come with the president's name attached.

The advantages of reliable timing and particular location

[27] Evidence linking short-term movements in real disposable income to social welfare expenditures is given in Richard P. Y. Li, "Public Policy and Short-Term Fluctuations in U.S. Voting Behavior: A Reformulation and Expansion," *Political Methodology*, 3 (1976), 49-70.

favor the employment of increased transfer payments over general macroeconomic strategies (tax cuts, increased spending) in the production of the electoral-economic cycle. Transfer payments, furthermore, have become increasingly important as they consume a larger and very substantial share of government expenditure. The conclusion is that general fiscal and monetary policy, while no doubt sometimes tilted as a result of electoral considerations, does not play a dominant role in the pre-election stimulation of the economy. This explains the lack of evidence linking tax cuts to election years. It also explains Lindbeck's decidedly mixed report on the entanglement of fiscal policy in the electoral cycle:

> We also find some examples of expansionary fiscal policies during booms immediately before general elections. Examples are Germany in 1965 and the UK in 1955 and 1965; the observation is somewhat obscured by the fact that some counter-examples, of restrictive actions immediately *before* general elections, can also be found, such as the increase in indirect taxes in Sweden in 1960 and in the UK in 1965, as well as the introduction of the surcharge in the US in 1968.

> Sometimes party-politics and balance of payments considerations seem to have interacted to form a go-stop cycle. Expansionary actions have been taken in booms, sometimes for party-political reasons. This has been followed by a period of strong inflationary tendencies with a deterioration in the balance of payments, which later has induced the authorities to take restrictive actions; in some cases these restrictive actions have been pursued long into the next recession, partly because speculations in the exchange rate had already started. The famous British *go-stop cycle* seems to be to some extent the result of such a political-balance-of-payments cycle. Something similar seems to have happened in Germany in connection with the expansionary policies in 1958 and 1963-4, in Italy in

1963-4, in France in connection with the expansionary policy in 1955-6 and 1965, as well as in Sweden in connection with the expansionary policies in 1964-5.[28]

At least partially implicated in the election-year stimulation of the economy are many different agencies and groups —those who make economic policy, those who monitor the budget and rate of spending, those who pass legislation increasing beneficiary payments in an election year, and those who determine the money supply. When the charge of "election-year economics" is made against some of these actors, the reply is often that the decision to spend more faster was "bipartisan," reached without partisan disagreement, and that may often be the case. Translated, the reply means that the agency will help stimulate the economy for any administration, regardless of party. Few governmental agencies have an interest in *not* stimulating the economy in an election year. Most hold an interest in positively helping with election-year stimulation, although the reasons behind that interest vary from agency to agency. The representative in Congress supports the biennial increases in beneficiary payments because such support may be helpful in the reelection campaign, because it is difficult to vote against beneficiary legislation helping a specific group of voters in an election year, or because of the belief that election-year prosperity is good for all incumbents regardless of party—and, besides, in the case of some beneficiary legislation, the increased benefits start before the election and the increased costs start after the election. The agency that accelerates its administration of economic stimulus may do so to stay out of trouble with the White House, to parley an election-year increase into permanent expansion, or to maintain its long-run independence by short-run assistance to those who might most immediately threaten its independence—that is, current officeholders (who, with the usual incumbency advantage, can be expected to be back after the election). Given these diverse goals held

28 Lindbeck, "Fiscal Policy," p. 28.

by these diverse participants in election-year economic stimulation, those economic models of politics that begin—and sometimes end—by assuming that a single unit called the "government" chooses an optimal economic path consistent with maximizing its expected vote in the next election appear simplistic indeed. The diverse ends are not explained by the common means.

Even those not in power become implicated in election-year upturns. During the election campaign, nonincumbent candidates (particularly Democrats) find themselves in the ironic posture of advocating stimulative economic policies as correctives for what they attack as the failed policies of the incumbent Republicans. Incumbents, proclaiming they are also keeping a keen eye on inflation and government spending, are happy to oblige. Such was the pattern of the pre-election bidding in the 1972 social security increase.

The maintenance of the electoral-economic cycle also acts as a constraint on the range of choice in economic policy-making. Specifically, austerity measures and deflationary policies are less likely to be pursued in election years than in years without elections.[29] Similarly, government agencies, even if unable to exploit the pre-election expansionary climate, can effectively fight proposals to cut their budgets during election years. A former chairman of the Council of Economic Advisers reported in an interview that the discount rate of austerity policies was so high in election years as to exclude such policies from serious consideration. He also said that the council "never won an argument" with the Department of Agriculture in an election year, because the White House did not want to cut back benefits at that time. Similarly, closings of military bases and veterans hospitals are initiated in odd-numbered years. So-called showcase pro-

[29] Included in a set of norms held by economic policy-makers is "Do not ask for a tax increase in an election year" (Lawrence C. Pierce, *The Politics of Fiscal Policy Formation* [Pacific Palisades, Calif.: Goodyear, 1971], p. 34). On the desires of incumbent presidents to receive greater discretionary tax authority, see Louis Fisher, *President and Congress* (New York: The Free Press, 1972), pp. 170-173.

grams also follow the political rhythm, surfacing in even-numbered years, particularly in the summer and fall.[30]

The constraints placed on economic policy in election years, although difficult to assess quantitatively (at least without the heroic assumptions required in large-scale macroeconomic simulations), may well be the strongest influence that elections have on macroeconomic policy.[31] Foregoing the hard cures of austerity policies in election years (even if economic conditions might require such measures) is probably easier on the consciences—and the professional reputations—of economic policy-makers than actively participating in positive actions that induce an election-year boom.

[30] The political targeting and election-year timing of federal programs under President Roosevelt is described by Gavin Wright, "The Political Economy of New Deal Spending: An Econometric Analysis," *Review of Economics and Statistics*, 56 (February 1974), 30-38. More recently, one particularly wasteful election-year showcase program was the $57 million "people-mover" in Morgantown, West Virginia. The project director reported "tremendous pressure" to have something to show before November 1972. Three weeks before the election the daughter of the president made a campaign visit to the project. Soon after the election, this Potemkin village was abandoned. (*New York Times*, April 13, 1974, pp. 1, 26.) The influence of election-year pressures in accelerating the development of methadone drug treatment whereby the "President set in motion one of the most unorthodox programs ever initiated by government —the financing of a national narcotics distribution intended to replace a dangerous form of drug addiction by a putatively benign one" is reported in Edward Jay Epstein, "The Krogh File—the Politics of 'Law and Order,'" *The Public Interest*, 39 (Spring 1975), 99-124, at p. 121; see also Epstein, *Agency of Fear* (New York: G. P. Putnam's Sons, 1977). On short-run patronage in relation to the electoral cycle in the Philippines, see Thomas C. Nowak, "The Philippines before Martial Law: A Study in Politics and Administration," *American Political Science Review*, 71 (June 1977), 522-539.

[31] ". . . the years in which the voters choose their Presidents tend to be times when a number of things do *not* happen in Washington that very likely would except for the national campaign" (Warren Weaver, Jr., "Political Fever Is Causing Washington Malaise . . . ," *New York Times*, August 15, 1976, p. E-4). Weaver's analysis provides some twenty examples of election-year delays in foreign-policy initiatives, legislation, and even filling vacant administration positions.

Given all the forces promoting election-year economic stimulation, why is every presidential election year *not* like 1972? What prevents most administrations from going all out? What limits the deployment of economic policies based solely on optimizing economic performance at election time?

First, the conditions that most incite election year economic stimulation—those, according to our evidence, prevailing when a powerful incumbent seeks re-election—often do not obtain. Aging, mortality, resignation, and constitutional limitations on re-election moderate the electoral-economic cycle. Second, election-year politics itself limits how grossly and crudely political economic policy can be. Incumbents must protect themselves against campaign charges of inflationary policies, big spending, and the political manipulation of economic policy.[32] Even increased spending, furthermore, must have some basis in reality; increases cannot be justified merely by the fact of the election. Third, not all of those deciding economic policy single-mindedly pursue the pure interests of the incumbent executive. Economic policy-makers often have interests and constituencies quite different from those of the incumbent administration. Economic advisers may feel that they have to answer to their professional colleagues or their potential future employers in addition to their political benefactors. The upshot may be more "responsible," depoliticized economic policies.[33] Similarly, the interest of central bankers, members of the national legislature, and the bureaucracy may diverge

---

[32] For example, although the economic lull shortly before 1976 election disturbed President Ford's advisers, they did find one small bright spot: "It proves that we did not blow up the economy to win the election," said William Seidman, the White House economic adviser (*Newsweek*, October 18, 1976; pp. 92, 97).

[33] A sensitive account of the role of the professional economist in advising the president is Arthur M. Okun, *The Political Economy of Prosperity* (Washington, D.C.: The Brookings Institution, 1969). See also the discussion of former presidential advisers in "How Political Must the Council of Economic Advisers Be?" *Challenge*, 17 (March-April 1974), 28-42.

from the electoral needs of the executive, thereby limiting their contributions to election-year economic stimulation.[34] Fourth, all the factors that impede the attainment of any desired economic objective—external shocks, inertia, policy failures, unanticipated consequences, ignorance—also work to limit election-year economic optimizing. Fifth, the incumbent executive's character—what else can it be called?—certainly must make a difference. The extremes of 1972 were special because Richard Nixon was special. Finally, it is worth remembering that election-based economic targets vary from administration to administration. Politicians, mainly as a function of their location on the left-right ideological spectrum, vary in their theories about what it is the electorate wants delivered in terms of economic policy and

[34] This point is developed, usually from a conservative or at least an anti-big-government perspective, in much recent work. See Keith Acheson and John F. Chant, "The Choice of Monetary Instruments and the Theory of Bureaucracy," *Public Choice*, 12 (Spring 1972), 13-34; James M. Buchanan, *Public Finance in the Democratic Process* (Chapel Hill: University of North Carolina Press, 1967); James M. Buchanan and Richard E. Wagner, *Democracy in Deficit* (New York: Academic Press, 1977); William A. Niskanen, "Bureaucracy and the Interests of Bureaucrats," *Journal of Law and Economics*, 18 (December 1975), 617-643; and Randall B. Ripley and Grace A. Franklin, *Congress, the Bureaucracy, and Public Policy* (Homewood, Ill.: Dorsey, 1976). Mayhew, *Congress: The Electoral Connection*, p. 31, n. 46, considers the case of extreme divergence between the executive and members of the legislative branch:

Do marginal congressmen—or members generally—of the party not in control of the presidency try to sabotage the economy? Of course they must not appear to do so, but there are "respectable" ways of acting. How about Republicans in the Eightieth Congress with their tax cutting in time of inflation? Or Democrats with their spending programs under President Nixon—also in a time of inflation? The answer is probably no. It would have to be shown that the same congressmen's actions differ under presidencies of different parties, and they probably do not. Strategies like this not only require duplicity, they require a vigorous consciousness of distant effects of a sort that is foreign to the congressional mentality.

performance. Certainly everyone wants prosperity—but the character of that prosperity and the particular mix of economic trade-offs presented to the voters are determined, as we shall see, by political ideology and by the objective economic problems facing the administration.[35]

[35] The findings describing the electoral-economic cycle possibly have some implications for economic forecasting. The known periodicity of the cycle may help to predict future movements of the economy. Acknowledgment of the occurrence of elections may improve the predictive records of macroeconomic models. Investment strategists might consider that the ups and downs of the stock market have reflected the pattern of the presidential side of the electoral economic cycle, with substantially more bullish performances in the two years before the presidential election than in the two years following it. From 1946 to 1973, the average return on Standard and Poor's 500 stocks was 14.8 percent in the two years before the presidential election compared to 10.0 percent in the two years after the election. Several other tabulations of stock-market performance are consistent with these results. I leave it to others to make any projections to future years. I am indebted to John Bennett, Senior Vice President, Putnam Management Company, Boston, for providing these figures.

3
A Note on Elections and the International Economy

In recent years the economies of the world's capitalist democracies have displayed more or less parallel business cycles, a fact giving rise to many theories about the nature of economic interdependence. Most national economies participated in the booms of 1968-1970 and 1972-1973, the upward drift of 1976, as well as the slump of 1974-1975. The ups and downs of the major capitalist economies have, in the jargon, become "synchronized."

That other economies expanded with the U.S. presidential cycle (in 1968, 1972, and 1976) hints at an international electoral-economic cycle. Does our basic principle

> When you think economics, think elections;
> When you think elections, think economics

offer any help here? Can macroeconomic fluctuations at an international level be explained, at least in part, by the electoral calendar?

At hand is a simple but striking set of data for the seven largest capitalist economies: Canada, France, Germany, Italy, Japan, the United Kingdom, and the United States. Table 3-1 shows the median annual growth rate in real GNP per capita for these countries over the eighteen years from 1959 to 1976 in relation to elections. This substantial amount of economic and electoral experience follows a clear pattern:

1. The GNP growth rate in election years is nearly double the rate in years without elections in all countries except Italy. The median election-year growth rate is 4.3 percent; for years without elections, 2.4 percent. (In Table 3-1, compare columns 1 and 2 with column 4.)

TABLE 3-1

MEDIAN ANNUAL GROWTH RATES (PERCENT), REAL GNP PER CAPITA,
ELECTION YEARS AND YEARS WITHOUT ELECTIONS, 1959-1976

	Election Years			
	1 *Country's election and U.S. election in same year*	*2* *Country's election only*	*3* *U.S. election only*	*4* *No election in country or in U.S.*
Canada	4.3	4.1	4.3	1.8
France	4.4	4.7	5.5	4.3
Germany	2.8	4.4	6.9	2.4
Italy	2.3	9.6	3.8	4.6
Japan	10.7	9.3	12.8	6.8
United Kingdom	4.9	2.5	2.9	1.5
United States			4.0	2.1
Overall	4.3	4.6	4.3	2.4

2. Election-year expansions in the United States economy appear to spill over to other economies. The growth rates in real GNP in *other* countries are nearly double in the years of U.S. presidential elections compared to years without elections in the U.S. or the country itself. (Compare column 3 with column 4. Italy remains the one exception.) A presidential election in the United States is nearly as effective in producing accelerated economic growth in Canada, France, Germany, Japan, and the United Kingdom as an election in the country itself. (Compare columns 1 and 2 with column 3.)

Elections, then, partially account for yearly fluctuations in real growth rates in the major capitalist countries. Can the occurrence of elections also help explain the increasing synchronization of economic swings in the major economies? A convincing investigation of this question would require the specification and estimation of a model for a set of open economies, but even without such a model we can pursue a most intriguing clue.

Figure 3-1 compiles the dates of elections for the seven countries from 1959 to 1976. Note the increasing clustering of elections in recent years, particularly the heaping of elections (kyphosis again) in the eleven months from May 1972 to March 1973 when six of the seven countries had national elections. Thus this election boom matched the economic boom.

In recent years, moreover, the major capitalist countries have moved to a U.S. electoral calendar. Before 1971, elections in Canada, France, Italy, Germany, Japan, and the United Kingdom were actually more likely to take place in odd-numbered years than in even-numbered years. From 1971 to 1976, however, only a single election in these six countries was held in an odd-numbered year (and that hardly counts as a contrary case, since it was the French election of March 1973 at the peak of the 1972-1973 international boom). The dates of the thirty-five elections in the six countries break down into this remarkable table:

| | Elections held in | |
	even-numbered year	odd-numbered year
1959-1970	9	13
1971-1976	11	1

Including the dates of U.S. elections shows the tremendous electoral pressure recently placed on even-numbered years by the seven largest capitalist countries:

| | Elections held in | |
	even-numbered year	odd-numbered year
1959-1970	15	13
1971-1976	14	1

FIGURE 3-1
ELECTION DATES, 1959–1976

Country marks	1959	1960	1961	1962	1963	1964	1965	1966
(above axis)	B	J / U	G	U- / C F	C / I / J	B / U	C / G F	B / U-
Quarters	1 2 3 4	1 2 3 4	1 2 3 4	1 2 3 4	1 2 3 4	1 2 3 4	1 2 3 4	1 2 3 4

Country marks	1967	1968	1969	1970	1971	1972	1973	1974	1975	1976
(above axis)	J / F	C / I / F U	F G J	B U-		C / G / J — I U	F	B — CU- / J B		J G / I U
Quarters	1 2 3 4	1 2 3 4	1 2 3 4	1 2 3 4	1 2 3 4	1 2 3 4	1 2 3 4	1 2 3 4	1 2 3 4	1 2 3 4

Date of Election

B = Britain
C = Canada
F = France
G = Germany

I = Italy
J = Japan
U = United States presidential elections
U- = United States midterm congressional elections

Election years, as we have seen, tend to produce economic expansions in many countries.[1] With the synchronization of electoral calendars in large capitalist democracies, we have a recipe for an international boom and bust cycle: "If sufficiently many large countries pursue expansionary economic policies, there will be a pronounced international boom, and if the governments, alarmed at the resulting inflation, drastically re-cast their policies in a restrictive direction, there will be a large international downturn."[2]

What may in part lie behind the appearance of economic interdependence, then, may simply be the internationalization of the U.S. electoral-economic cycle. Like any other powerful external determinant of economic outcomes, such a cycle reduces the possibility and scope of the democratic control of economic policy in each country caught up in the international electoral-economic cycle.[3]

[1] Similar (but independent) findings have been reported in the OECD report, *Towards Full Employment and Price Stability* (Paris, June 1977). Recent electoral-economic synchronicity has perhaps flourished because of the increased flexibility in short-run economic management now afforded by the very substantial increases in reserve assets in the OECD countries since 1970. Official international liquidity more than doubled from 1970 to 1974. (*OECD Economic Outlook*, 17 [July 1975], 73-75.) The growth in reserve assets may provide the economic base for short-term election-year expansion.

[2] Assar Lindbeck, "Business Cycles, Politics and International Economic Dependence," *Skandinaviska Enskilda Banken Quarterly*, 2 (1975), 60.

[3] Richard N. Cooper, *The Economics of Interdependence: Economic Policy in the Atlantic Community* (New York: McGraw-Hill, 1968), pp. 148-173; Robert A. Dahl and Edward R. Tufte, *Size and Democracy* (Stanford: Stanford University Press, 1973), pp. 128-142. As the 1976 international election season opened, one observer of the British economy made it all very clear:

. . . what happens to Britain will be very much affected by what happens in the giant economies of the U.S., Germany, and Japan [all having elections in 1976]. If these three countries, which between them account for a fifth of British exports, remain depressed this year, the British economy will certainly not recover. If they revive, the key question for Mr Healey will be how fast to allow the revival to feed through into the British economy. One of the

69

These results suggest a partial remedy for the increasingly unstable oscillations of the major capitalist economies. The way to desynchronize economies is to desynchronize elections and to stop riding the U.S. electoral-economic cycle. If smoothing the international economic cycle were the sole concern, then a good many more elections should be held in odd-numbered years and especially in the year before the U.S. presidential elections. That is surely less to ask of incumbent politicians than to ask them to stop heating up their country's economy in election years.

---

nastier facts of life is that the level of unemployment in Britain this year will depend largely on the whim of other countries' electorates. (Frances Cairncross, "Polls Hold the Key to Recovery," *Guardian*, December 29, 1975, p. 12.)

4

Political Parties and Macroeconomic Outcomes

Although the synchronization of economic fluctuations with the electoral cycle often preoccupies political leaders, the real force of political influence on macroeconomic performance comes in the determination of economic priorities. Here the ideology and platform of the political party in power dominate. Just as the electoral calendar helps set the timing of policy, so the ideology of political leaders shapes the substance of economic policy.

POLITICAL PARTIES AND THEIR ECONOMIC PRIORITIES

Political parties differ on what they consider desirable economic policy. Parties of the Right favor low rates of taxation and inflation along with modest and balanced government budgets, oppose income equalization, and will trade greater unemployment for less inflation most of the time. Parties of the Left, in contrast, favor income equalization and lower unemployment, larger government budgets, and will accept increased rates of inflation in order to reduce unemployment. Such differences between Left and Right appear in country after country.[1]

---

[1] Good evidence on this obvious point comes from a survey of experts in 8 countries; see E. S. Kirschen et al., *Economic Policy in Our Time*, (Amsterdam: North-Holland Publishing, 1964), 1: 224-229; detailed country-by-country evidence is reported in volumes 2 and 3 of Kirschen et al. Other reports are in E. S. Kirschen, ed., *Economic Policies Compared: West and East*, vol. 1, *General Theory* (Amsterdam: North-Holland Publishing, 1974). See also Seymour E. Harris, *The Economics of the Political Parties* (New York: Macmillan, 1962); Bruno Frey and Lawrence J. Lau, "Towards a Mathematical Model of Government Behaviour," *Zeitschrift für Nation-*

In the United States, for example, the 1976 Democratic platform began its pledges on economic issues with the statement, "We do pledge a Government which will be committed to a fairer distribution of wealth, income and power."[2] And later: "The Democratic party has a long history of opposition to the undue concentration of wealth and economic power. It is estimated that about three-quarters of the country's total wealth is owned by one-fifth of the people. The rest of our population struggles to make ends meet in the face of rising prices and taxes." The platform dealt at length with economic matters, particularly unemployment, and the party pledged to support legislation that would make every responsible effort to reduce adult unemployment to 3 percent within four years—a promise, given its artful wording, that would not be hard to deliver on. Although the Democratic platform contained a brief section on inflation, overall references to unemployment outnumbered references to inflation by 48 to 30.

The 1976 Republican platform was very different. In its 65 pages, the word *unemployment* was used only once in the context of doing something about it, at a time when the unemployment rate had averaged 8 percent for two years,

---

alökonomie, 28 (1968), 355-380. Further major developments are in Douglas Hibbs, Jr., "Political Parties and Macroeconomic Policy," *American Political Science Review*, 71 (December 1977), 1467-1487; and Hibbs, "Economic Interest and the Politics of Macroeconomic Policy," Center for International Studies, M.I.T., January 1976.

[2] Quotations are from the full text of the party platforms: Democratic National Committee, *The National Democratic Platform 1976*, and Republic National Convention, *Platform*. Excerpts from the Democratic platform were printed in the *New York Times*, June 18, 1976, p. 12; from the Republican platform, *New York Times*, August 16, 1976, p. 16. See Richard L. Madden, "2 Party Platforms Show Sharp Contrast on Issues," *New York Times*, August 15, 1976, p. 1; and Henry A. Plotkin, "Issues in the 1976 Presidential Campaign," in Gerald M. Pomper et al., *The Election of 1976* (New York: McKay, 1977), pp. 35-53. The differences between the Democratic and Republican platforms on economic matters appear sharply contrasting relative to the range of policy options debated in the American political arena.

the highest level since the 1930s. That reference did not betray an excess of compassion for the jobless: "Republicans hope every American realizes that if we are permanently to eliminate high unemployment, it is essential to protect the integrity of our money. That means putting an end to deficit spending. The danger, sooner or later, is runaway inflation." Similar priorities were set in the preamble: "The Democrats' platform repeats the same thing on every page: More government, more spending, more inflation. Compare. This Republican platform says exactly the opposite—less government, less spending, less inflation. In other words, we want you to retain more of your own money, money that represents the worth of your labors, to use as you see fit for the necessities and conveniences of life."[3]

The parties' differences on distributional issues and on the suitable size, scope, and cost of national government were as striking as their differing sensitivities to inflation and unemployment. The Democrats made 87 clear references to matters of equity, income distribution, class differences, and opportunity compared to 25 similar mentions in the Republican platform. The parties diverged on the extent of government spending: the Republican platform contained 42 separate mentions of "federal spending," "big government," and

[3] Their differences extended to typographic style and how best to misquote Thomas Jefferson. In the convention versions of the platforms, the Democrats used "Government," the Republicans, "government." Compelled by the occasion of the bicentennial to mention the Declaration of Independence, both parties treated Jefferson's revolutionary words gingerly and with incomplete fidelity. The Democrats updated the Declaration by replacing "Men" with "persons" and "People": "That all persons are created equal, that they are endowed by their Creator with certain unalienable rights, that among these are Life, Liberty, and the Pursuit of Happiness—That to secure these rights, Governments are instituted among People, deriving their just powers from the consent of the governed." The Republicans ellipsized out the mention of equality, retained the gendered references, and had Jefferson taking a tough line: "It was our 'Declaration' which put the world and posterity on notice 'that Men are . . . endowed by their Creator with certain unalienable Rights' and that those rights must not be taken from those to whom God has given them."

"deficit spending" compared to 9 such references in the Democratic platform. Table 4-1 tabulates the words and phrases dealing with economic policy in the two platforms. It is clear that even what many consider to be the ideologically bland political parties of the United States display the classic differences between Left and Right on fundamental issues of economic policy—the distribution of wealth and income, the proper scope and cost of government, and the trade-off between inflation and unemployment.

The U.S. parties not only differ on economic issues; they differ more on economic issues than on other matters. A tabulation of specific pledges made in the Democratic and Republican platforms from 1944 to 1964 (1,399 pledges in all!) found that economic and labor issues showed the highest proportion of conflicting stands between the parties (the other issues were foreign affairs, defense, agriculture, resources, welfare, government, and civil rights).[4]

Party platforms and similar policy statements reveal the differences that divide the activists of the two parties. On some issues, elite-level differences do not percolate on down to each party's rank and file. On economic issues, however, the priorities asserted in each party's platform match up with the economic priorities held by each party's rank-and-file membership, as a significant variety of survey evidence confirms.[5] To take just one of many examples, a 1976 election-

[4] Gerald M. Pomper, *Elections in America* (New York: Dodd, Mead, 1971), pp. 192-195.

[5] Recent evidence for the United States is summarized in Arthur M. Okun, "Comments on Stigler's Paper," *American Economic Review*, 63 (May 1973), 172-177; and in Arthur H. Miller and Warren E. Miller, "Partisanship and Performance: 'Rational' Choice in the 1976 Presidential Elections," paper delivered at the annual meeting of the American Political Science Association, September 1977. For Britain, see James E. Alt, Bo Särlvik, and Ivor Crewe, "Partisanship and Policy Choice: Issue Preference in the British Electorate, February, 1974," *British Journal of Political Science*, 6 (July 1976), 273-290; David Butler and Donald Stokes, *Political Change in Britain*, 2nd ed. (New York: St. Martin's Press, 1974); and the two papers of Hibbs. Samuel Brittan, "The Economic Contradictions of Democracy," *British Journal of Political Science*, 5 (April 1975), at pp.

TABLE 4-1

NUMBER OF TIMES CERTAIN PHRASES DEALING WITH
ECONOMIC POLICY WERE USED IN THE DEMOCRATIC AND
REPUBLICAN PLATFORMS OF 1976

| | Number of times word used | |
	Democratic platform	Republican platform
Distributional Issues		
inequity, regressive, equitable, equal, equality, redistribution	30	15
opportunity	24	7
poor, poverty	23	3
Size and Cost of National Government		
federal spending, government spending	3	22
size, cost of government	2	11
deficit, deficit spending, balanced budget	4	9
taxes	37	45
private sector, private enterprise	3	10
Unemployment		
full employment	14	0
unemployment, unemployed, jobless	34	7
Inflation		
inflation, inflationary	18	14
price stability, stable prices, rising prices, soaring prices	12	3

day sample of voters inquired: "In your opinion, which is the more important problem facing the country today: finding jobs for people who are unemployed, holding down inflation, or are both equally important?"[6] Democratic and Republican voters divided as follows:

	Democrats	Republicans
Jobs more important	27%	11%
Inflation more important	18	36
Both equally important	53	51
Not sure	2	2
	100%	100%
	(6,297)	(3,712)

Data compiled by Arthur H. Miller and Warren E. Miller show that party members have diverged somewhat more on unemployment than inflation (Figure 4-1). Note that the public's concern is quite responsive to the objective economic conditions and that as those conditions become more trying, the partisan differences over economic priorities increase.

PARTY IDEOLOGY AND THE MAKING OF NATIONAL
ECONOMIC POLICY

The arguments and priorities advanced by party platforms are often the very same arguments and priorities that are

---

133-134, reports a public opinion poll showing that while explanations for the causes of British inflation differ among Labour, Liberal, and Conservative supporters, the electorate is perhaps even more confused than policy-makers and economists about the causes of inflation. Still more British evidence on party links to the inflation-unemployment nexus is contained in C.A.E. Goodhart and R. J. Bhansali, "Political Economy," *Political Studies*, 18 (March 1970), 43-106; but see also Bruno S. Frey and Hermann Garbers, " 'Politico-Econometrics'—On Estimation in Political Economy," *Political Studies*, 19 (September 1971), 316-320.

[6] The survey was conducted by NBC Election News, which interviewed 15,411 voters at the polls in randomly selected precincts. Additional information on the survey is given in the Appendix.

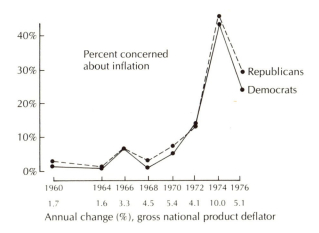

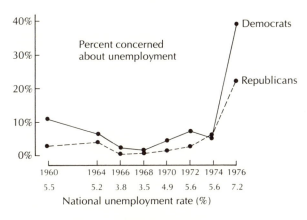

FIGURE 4-1
CONCERN ABOUT INFLATION AND UNEMPLOYMENT IN
RELATION TO POLITICAL PARTY AND OBJECTIVE
ECONOMIC CONDITIONS, 1960-1976

found at the heart of high-level economic policy-making. Many private memoranda on macroeconomic policy exchanged between the president and his advisers read almost exactly like a party platform (except for additional material on what interests support what position).[7] This is not surprising, since the same people sometimes wrote both.

The most important public document of macroeconomic policy is the annual volume combining the *Economic Report of the President* (a mix of a State of the Union message and a party platform) and *The Annual Report of the Council of Economic Advisers* (a detailed policy analysis addressed to policy-makers and to economists and their students). Some sense of the economic priorities expressed can be gained by counting how many times each report uses the words "unemployment" and "inflation." Such a count has been made for both the president's and the CEA reports for the 16 years of the Kennedy-Johnson-Nixon-Ford administrations. Although surely exemplifying barefoot empiricism, the tabulation does yield a crude, but objective and replicable measure of each report's relative emphasis on unemployment and inflation. The counts seem to catch the sense of the text. The three *Economic Reports of the President* signed by Gerald Ford, for example, mention unemployment 18 times and inflation 43 times, a reasonable reflection of the priorities disclosed in the full texts. (The unemployment/inflation ratio in the 1976 Republican platform was 7 to 17.)

The rates of usage of "unemployment" and "inflation" shown in Table 4-2 repay study, particularly in relation to

[7] This statement is based on a reading of several hundred White House memoranda dealing with the budget and economic policy. The documents were collected by John P. Crecine from the Truman, Eisenhower, Kennedy, and Johnson libraries. Some additional evidence and discussions of the role of partisan politics in economic policy-making are in Leonard S. Silk, "Truth vs. Partisan Political Purpose," *American Economic Review*, 62 (May 1972), 376-378; Harry G. Johnson, "Scholars as Public Adversaries: The Case of Economics," in his *On Economics and Society* (Chicago: University of Chicago Press, 1975), pp. 140-152; and the discussion of several economists who advised the president in "How Political Must the Council of Economic Advisers Be?" *Challenge*, 17 (March-April 1974), 28-42.

TABLE 4-2

"Unemployment" and "Inflation" Usage Rates in Annual Economic Reports of President and CEA

Date of report (each January)	Party of president	Usage rates: mentions per 10 pages				National economic conditions at time of report	
		President's Report		CEA Report			
		"unemployment"	"inflation"	"unemployment"	"inflation"	Unemployment rate	Inflation rate
1977	Republican	4.9	23.2	10.0	8.5	7.7%	5.1%
1976	Republican	16.1	26.8	7.9	7.9	8.5%	9.3%
1975	Republican	9.3	16.7	12.7	7.3	5.6%	10.0%
1974	Republican	7.0	18.3	2.3	3.9	4.9%	5.8%
1973	Republican	12.8	34.0	5.2	8.2	5.6%	4.1%
1972	Republican	18.8	29.2	5.4	8.2	5.9%	5.1%
1971	Republican	20.0	38.5	5.0	5.3	4.9%	5.4%
1970	Republican	10.8	21.7	4.4	7.3	3.5%	5.0%
1969	Democratic	5.7	3.8	5.7	2.8	3.6%	4.5%
1968	Democratic	5.6	2.0	3.1	2.6	3.8%	2.9%
1967	Democratic	6.0	3.0	5.2	1.7	3.8%	3.3%
1966	Democratic	7.7	5.5	4.7	2.7	4.5%	2.2%
1965	Democratic	4.8	5.4	6.2	1.1	5.2%	1.6%
1964	Democratic	9.4	6.3	3.8	1.9	5.7%	1.5%
1963	Democratic	9.2	3.6	4.4	2.5	5.5%	1.8%
1962	Democratic	13.0	3.2	9.0	3.1	6.7%	0.9%

the political party of the president and to the actual rates of unemployment and inflation. Considerable consistency and structure, both within and between years, is evident in the data.

Tables 4-3 and 4-4 display multiple regressions accounting for the year-to-year variation in the U/I ratio

$$\frac{\text{number of mentions of ``unemployment''}}{\text{number of mentions of ``inflation''}}$$

TABLE 4-3

CEA Annual Reports, 1962-1977, Mentions of Unemployment and Inflation in Relation to Economic Conditions, the Political Party of the President, and the Special Interest of the Ford CEA in the Unemployment Problem

	Regression coefficients and (t-values) for 4 regressions			
	1	*2*	*3*	*4*
Economic conditions	.69 (3.13)		.21 (.80)	.22 (.97)
Political party of president		.98 (4.59)	.81 (2.66)	1.04 (3.72)
Ford CEA				.64 (2.35)
R^2	.41	.60	.62	.74

The regressions have the form

$$ln(UM/IM) = \beta_0 + \beta_1 ln(\bar{U}/\bar{I}) + \beta_2 P + \beta_3 F$$

where *UM* and *IM* are the number of mentions of unemployment and inflation in the CEA *Report* issued in January of year i; $\bar{U}$ is the national unemployment rate (averaged over years i, $i-1$, and $i-2$) and $\bar{I}$ is the implicit price deflator for the GNP (also averaged over three years); P is the political party of the incumbent president (Democrat = 1, Republican = 0); and F is equal to one during the years of the Ford CEA and zero otherwise.

in the CEA *Report* and the *Economic Report of the President.*[8] These simple regressions pick up about three-fourths of the variance in the U/I ratio over the four administrations. Furthermore, it is the case that:

1. Democrats—both presidents and professional economists serving on the Council of Economic Advisers—differ quite sharply from Republican presidents and their economic advisers. Democratic reports mentioned unemployment about twice as often as inflation; Republican reports mentioned inflation 1.7 times more often than unemployment. For the CEA reports, political party accounts for up to 60 percent of the statistical variation in the U/I ratio over the years; for the president's reports, political party accounts for up to 77 percent of the variation in U/I. Note also the great shift in economic priorities between the last Johnson report and the first Nixon report, even though objective economic conditions (measured by the unem-

TABLE 4-4

ECONOMIC REPORT OF THE PRESIDENT, 1962-1977,
MENTIONS OF UNEMPLOYMENT AND INFLATION IN RELATION
TO ECONOMIC CONDITIONS AND THE POLITICAL PARTY
OF THE PRESIDENT

	Regression coefficients and (t-values) for 3 regressions		
	1	2	3
Economic conditions	.88 (3.06)		.047 (.18)
Political party of president		1.43 (6.81)	1.40 (4.55)
R^2	.40	.77	.77

[8] Actually the logarithm of the ratio is used so that equal changes in either mentions of inflation or of unemployment receive equal weight.

ployment rate and the change in the GNP deflator) changed very little (see Table 4-2).

2. The objective economic reality—at least that measured by the actual unemployment/inflation ratio prevailing around the time of the reports—may also have something to do with the economic priorities expressed in the reports. The role of prevailing economic conditions in determining the U/I ratio does appear, however, to be rather modest at times (at least relative to the influence of political party), and several of the relevant regression coefficients are small, substantively and statistically insignificant. Several different measures of objective economic conditions were tried in multiple regressions similar to those of Tables 4-3 and 4-4 but none performed as well as the measure used here.[9]

3. The *Reports* of the president and of the CEA have been roughly in tune; the correlation between the U/I ratios in each is 0.60. This connection seems mainly to be the consequence of their common party affiliation; little correlation remains once party is taken into account. Several councils have diverged quite considerably from the economic priorities of the White House. In all three of its reports, the Ford CEA displayed much greater interest than the president in the problem of unemployment (Tables 4-2 and 4-3). The 1965 council also placed heavy emphasis on unemployment, even compared to Democratic councils.

Political party ideology, then, contributed very much to the determination of economic priorities expressed in the *Economic Report of the President* and in the *CEA Annual*

[9] For example, $ln(U/I)$ for the year reviewed by the report does less well than $ln(\bar{U}/\bar{I})$. There is a collinearity problem here, since the Democrats faced some high unemployment rates in the early 1960s and the Republicans high inflation rates in the early 1970s. The correlation between party and $ln(\bar{U}/\bar{I})$ is 0.70. Thus the estimates of the relative influence of political party and objective economic conditions may be somewhat unreliable. Further, some difficulties in model specification arise, since the policies advocated in the reports may in fact affect unemployment and inflation during the year of the reports (a year included in calculating $\bar{U}$ and $\bar{I}$).

Report from 1962 to 1977. Democrats were sensitive to unemployment; Republicans to inflation. As Arthur Okun has written: "When the chips were down, the Democrats have taken their chances on inflation and the Republicans on unemployment and recession. For a generation, every major mistake in economic policy under a Democratic president has taken the form of overstimulating the economy and every major mistake under a Republican president of overrestraining it."[10] Furthermore, political party ideology has shaped economic priorities—by our measures at any rate—far more than the objective economic conditions prevailing at the time of the reports.[11] Macroeconomic policy was apparently made more in response to the outputs of the political system (that is, what party had won the presidency) than to the objective performance of the economy. Perhaps that is as it should be in a democracy.

POLITICAL PARTIES, SOCIAL CLASS, AND ECONOMIC POLICY PREFERENCES

The divergent economic policy preferences of different political parties are rooted in the differences in their membership. In most countries, most parties are at least partially class-based, with poorer citizens favoring parties of the Left and the richer the parties of the Right. The strength of the bond between class and party varies from country to country.[12] In the United States, the link—of medium strength compared to other countries—has endured for many dec-

[10] Okun, "Comments on Stigler's Paper," p. 175.

[11] Some parallel findings are reported in Bruce M. Russett and Elizabeth C. Hanson, *Interest and Ideology: The Foreign Policy Beliefs of American Businessmen* (San Francisco: W. H. Freeman, 1975).

[12] Robert R. Alford, *Party and Society* (Chicago: Rand McNally, 1963); and Richard Rose, ed., *Electoral Behavior: A Comparative Handbook* (New York: The Free Press, 1974) provide cross-national comparisons of class polarization. See also David R. Cameron, "Consociation, Cleavage, and Realignment: Postindustrialization and Partisan Change in Eight European Nations," paper delivered at the annual meeting of the American Political Science Association, September, 1974.

ades. Since 1936 (when survey evidence first became available), the poorest fourth of the electorate has typically voted about 20 to 25 percentage points more Democratic than the richest fourth. Although hardly as invariable as the tie between class and party, class polarization in voting choices has appeared in every presidential election for which we have data, with a maximum difference of 40 percentage points between rich and poor in support for Truman in 1948 and a minimum difference of about 5 to 10 percentage points in support of the Democratic candidates running against Nixon in 1968 and 1972.[13] In 1976, when the salience of economic issues was fairly high, voters whose family income was less than $5,000 went 68 percent for Carter—compared to 42 percent among those with a family income exceeding $25,000. Economic policy preferences also prove to be partially class-based, with poorer citizens favoring efforts to reduce unemployment and richer citizens favoring efforts to reduce inflation.[14] For example, in the 1976 survey:

	Family income less than $5,000	Family income more than $25,000
Jobs more important	35%	13%
Inflation more important	19	29
Both equally important	42	57
Not sure	4	1
	100%	100%
	(981)	(2,703)

[13] Everett Carll Ladd, Jr., with Charles D. Hadley, *Transformations of the American Party System* (New York: W. W. Norton, 1975), pp. 72-74; Richard F. Hamilton, *Class and Politics in the United States* (New York: Wiley, 1972); and David Knoke, *Change and Continuity in American Politics: The Social Bases of Political Parties* (Baltimore: The Johns Hopkins University Press, 1976).

[14] Hibbs, "Economic Interest," and Eva Mueller, "Public Attitudes Toward Fiscal Programs," *Quarterly Journal of Economics*, 77 (May 1963), 210-235.

As their platforms indicated, the parties and candidates in the 1976 campaign clashed over economic priorities, providing product differentiation in the electoral marketplace. Those conflicts served to attract different constituencies to each party and candidate. The rates at which voters of differing party affiliation and economic priorities supported Carter or Ford are shown in the election-day survey reported in Table 4-5. In 1976, as usual, the vote divided sharply by party—but, in addition, the voters' macroeconomic priorities strongly influenced their choice. Even among Democrats (where he did quite well), Carter ran 13 percentage points better among those placing higher priority on unemployment than on inflation, and 10 percentage points better among the relatively modest number of Republicans who put unem-

TABLE 4-5

1976 PRESIDENTIAL VOTE IN RELATION TO THE VOTER'S
PARTY AFFILIATION, ECONOMIC PRIORITIES, AND INCOME

		What is the more important problem: finding jobs for people who are unemployed, holding down inflation, or are both equally important?		
Percent vote for Carter		*Jobs more important*	*Both equally important*	*Inflation more important*
Democrats		92%	84%	79%
Independents		71%	47%	28%
Republicans		15%	7%	5%
			Income		
Percent vote for Carter	*less than $5,000*	*$5,000-$10,000*	*$10,000-$15,000*	*$15,000-$25,000*	*greater than $25,000*
Democrats	93%	88%	87%	83%	81%
Independents	61%	55%	47%	44%	42%
Republicans	12%	7%	9%	8%	6%

Percentage bases:							
1751	3191	1035	513	1181	1572	1619	836
534	2314	869	171	471	907	1266	827
477	1988	1354	228	516	842	1202	904

ployment above inflation compared to those more concerned about inflation. Particularly striking in Table 4-5 is the influence of economic policy preferences on voters without a party affiliation. Independents who gave unemployment higher priority than inflation resembled hard-core Democrats, voting 71 percent for Carter. In contrast, those Independents rating inflation over unemployment were quite committed to the Republican ticket, voting 72 percent for Ford. The economic issue appears to have cut most deeply among those for whom the traditional guide for deciding how to vote—party identification—was absent. Economic policy preferences, as we have already seen, are partially encapsulated in party affiliation.[15] As the ties of party weaken and the ties of class persist, explicit economic priorities become a more dominant component in electoral choice.

Among the followers of each political party, the voters' choice in the presidential election was more closely related (by just a bit) to the voters' economic policy preferences than to the voters' income level. It may be, then, that investigation of the link between the vote and the economic policy preferences of voters would illuminate the character of changes in the relationship between social class and the vote. For example, the decline in class polarization in the elections of 1968 and 1972 followed by an increase in 1976 may simply reflect the muting of issues of economic priorities in 1968 and 1972 and the increased importance of economic priorities—particularly given the high levels of unemploy-

[15] Similar evidence, sometimes linking policy images of the parties to votes, is reported for 10 elections in Morris P. Fiorina, "Economic Conditions and National Elections: A Micro-Analysis," manuscript, 1976. V. O. Key's findings in his *The Responsible Electorate* (Cambridge, Mass.: Harvard University Press, 1966) on issue voting are largely based on relationships between citizens' views on *economic* issues and their vote. Disentangling the voters' party affiliation, issue views, and perceptions (possibly quite selective and biased) of candidates' stands on issues is impossible to do with any rigor. On this, see Richard A. Brody and Benjamin I. Page, "Comment: The Assessment of Policy Voting," *American Political Science Review*, 66 (June 1972), 450-458.

ment and inflation—in 1976. Changes in class polarization of electoral choice are largely a function of the salience of class-related economic issues in the election campaign. The salience of economic issues is in turn determined by the objective economic conditions of the time, the way in which those conditions affect specific voters, the other political issues at hand, and the decisions of politicians about what issues to emphasize, or indeed to create.

The strength of these relationships between class, party, party ideology, and electoral choice varies somewhat from country to country and from decade to decade.[16] Other conflicts—between ethnic groups, regions, and religions—sometimes dominate class-related economic concerns. Still, the ties between class, party, party ideology, and voting are among the most enduring correlations found in political life. Madison wrote in Federalist No. 10:

> The diversity in the faculties of men, from which the rights of property originate, is not less an insuperable obstacle to a uniformity of interests. The protection of these faculties is the first object of government. From the protection of different and unequal faculties of acquiring property, the possession of different degrees and kinds of property immediately results; and from the influence of these on the sentiments and views of the respective proprietors ensues a division of society into different interests and parties . . . the most common and durable source of factions has been the various and unequal distribution of property. Those who hold and those who are without property have ever formed distinct interests in society. Those who are creditors, and those who are debtors, fall under a like discrimination. A landed interest, a manufacturing interest, a mercantile interest, a moneyed interest, with many lesser interests, grow up of necessity in civilized nations, and divide them into different classes, actuated by different sentiments and views. The regulation of these various and

[16] See Richard Rose, "Comparability in Electoral Studies," in *Electoral Behavior*, pp. 3-25, for some quantitative assessments.

interfering interests forms the principal task of modern legislation and involves the spirit of party and faction in the necessary and ordinary operations of government.

CONSEQUENCES: POLITICAL PARTIES AND MACROECONOMIC OUTCOMES

Several sociologists and journalists during the 1950s and early 1960s promoted the ideology that ideological ideas had faded away, that the differences between the potential governing parties were usually small, and that the big ideological disputes over economic issues had ended. Political ideology, it was asserted, played little role in the practical management of the modern economy. The arguments played on the vagueness of their key terms and possessed little theoretical rigor. Anthony Downs did, however, develop a systematic set of ideas, based on sensible notions about how parties might rationally exploit knowledge about the distribution of voter opinion to pursue votes, that suggested that political parties (in a two-party system at least) would not seek to differentiate themselves ideologically from one another. The incentives apparently operated mainly to encourage parties to blur their platforms and move toward nearly identical ideological positions:

> Parties in a two-party system deliberately change their platforms so that they resemble one another; whereas parties in a multi-party system try to remain as ideologically distinct from each other as possible. . . . In a two-party system, it is rational for each party to encourage voters to be irrational by making its platform vague and ambiguous . . . an enormous overlapping of moderate policies. . . . Thus political rationality leads parties in a two-party system to becloud their policies in a fog of ambiguity.[17]

[17] Anthony Downs, *An Economic Theory of Democracy* (New York: Harper & Bros., 1957), pp. 115, 135, and 136. Cf. Donald A. Wittman, "Parties as Utility Maximizers," *American Political Science Review*, 67 (June 1973), 490-498.

As a result of the lack of differentiation between parties, the theory goes, voters would have to make their choices not on issues but on other grounds.

If this argument means that the economic ideologies, platforms, and policy statements of various political parties cannot be systemically distinguished from one another, then the evidence does not support the key deduction from the Downsian party model. Policy statements ranging from party platforms to the sophisticated policy analysis of the CEA *Reports* all manifest clear partisan divisions. The differences have been there for many years. Voters often detect—and act upon—the differences in party economic policy because it is in their economic interest to do so.

It might be imagined, however, that political parties diverge mainly over rhetoric, generating a pseudo-partisanship to appease ideologues or to fool voters. Such a charade would ultimately be exposed in the actual conduct of macroeconomic policy when the governing party faced the presumably technical, practical, and managerial problems of modern economic control. By one important test, a fairly broad consensus in the practice of economic policy can be found: a newly governing political party rarely throws out the major economic reforms initiated by the party it has displaced. Party turnover has not deflected the income tax, social security, unemployment compensation, health insurance, and the rich variety of subsidies to special interests once such programs were initiated and had acquired a momentum and logic of their own.[18]

What difference, then, does party ideology make in the determination of economic outcomes? To what extent are the economic platforms of the political parties realized? Theory and evidence are both in short supply here; the "effect of parties on policy-making is probably the most poorly investigated topic in the entire vast literature on political parties."[19]

[18] See Robert A. Dahl and Charles E. Lindblom, *Politics, Economics, and Welfare* (New York: Harper & Row, 1953), pp. 300-302, for a discussion of party alternation and stable policies.

[19] Hugh Heclo, *Modern Social Politics in Britain and Sweden* (New Haven: Yale University Press, 1974), p. 294, n. 6.

The main theoretical statement is again that of Downs, a quite different face of *An Economic Theory of Democracy* than the theory of two-party blurring. Downs concludes that "political parties tend to carry out as many of their promises as they can whenever they are elected."[20] It is, after all, only rational:

> In our model, it is necessary for each party's ideology to bear a consistent relation to its actions and to develop without repudiating the party's former acts. Any other procedure makes rational voting nearly impossible; hence voters impute value to parties with these traits. To win votes, all parties are forced by competition to be relatively honest and responsible in regard to both policies and ideologies.[21]

Some evidence is required. The experiences of several democracies offer data bearing on the association between the governing political party's economic principles and ongoing macroeconomic policy and performance.

Fulfillment of U.S. party platforms. According to Gerald Pomper's extensive tabulations of the six platforms of each party from 1944 to 1964 and of the policies enacted during that period, the party that won control of the White House managed to deliver on 84 percent of their specific platform pledges dealing with economic issues. While a number of promises were policies that both parties agreed on (raising the minimum wage, for example), it did make a difference who won the election; only 53 percent of the losing party's economic pledges came to pass.[22]

---

[20] Downs, *An Economic Theory of Democracy*, p. 300.

[21] Ibid., p. 113. Further developments are found in, among many others, Peter Bernholz, "Economic Policies in a Democracy," *Kyklos*, 19 (1966), 48-80; Brian M. Barry, *Sociologists, Economists and Democracy* (London: Collier-Macmillan, 1970), chapter 7; and Bruno S. Frey and Friedrich Schneider, "On the Modelling of Politico-Economic Interdependence," *European Journal of Political Research*, 3 (1975), 339-360.

[22] Pomper, *Elections in America*, pp. 188-189; for modified views,

Social policy in Britain and Sweden. In his study of unemployment insurance, pensions, and retirement benefits, Hugh Heclo found continuing differences between Left and Right in their social policies:

> Conservative parties in both nations can be found generally promoting a more strictly contributory system and expressing a particular concern with the state of national finances (we may recall, for example, Swedish Conservative opinion on pensions and unemployment benefits in 1913, 1914, 1922, 1928, and 1933; and British Conservatives in 1898, 1906, 1925, and 1934). The Labor parties on the other hand have historically placed major emphasis on immediate relief of need and benefit adequacy (as in Sweden and Britain on the scope of pension proposals during the first decade of the century and unemployment insurance in the 1920s).

Party differences have persisted:

> One would, for example, have to be particularly obtuse not to recognize the important differences—in content and orientation—between British Labor and Conservative superannuation proposals in the 1950s and again in the 1960s, or between the superannuation plan adopted . . . by the Swedish Social Democrats against bourgeois parties' preferences.[23]

---

see Benjamin Ginsberg, "Elections and Public Policy," *American Political Science Review*, 68 (March 1976), 41-49, and Richard T. Winters, "Party Control and Policy Change," *American Journal of Political Science*, 20 (November 1976), 597-636.

[23] Heclo, *Modern Social Politics*, pp. 296-297. Heclo's account also emphasizes impediments to effective party control of social policy; see pp. 293-297. Further, the major source of policy innovation was neither parties nor politicians; it was the bureaucracy. The diversity of political variables available to account for the diversity of policies (as well as ways to describe policies) poses severe problems for making generalizations and developing cumulative understanding of political-economic interactions. For example, often *some* characteristic of the party system (or the political system) can be found to account for *some* economic policy. "It is a principle that

Inflation and unemployment in 12 countries. Comparative evidence linking the ideology of the dominant political party to policy choices in the inflation-unemployment trade-off is reported by Douglas Hibbs in his study of 12 OECD countries from 1945 to 1969:

> Nations in which Social Democratic and Labor parties have governed for most or much of the postwar period have generally experienced high rates of inflation. Conversely, low rates of inflation have prevailed in countries where center and right-wing parties have dominated the policy-making process. The reverse is true of the association between average unemployment and average Socialist-Labor executive participation. Comparatively low rates of unemployment characterize systems in which left-wing parties have regularly controlled the executive and high unemployment rates have been typical in systems governed primarily by center and right-wing parties.[24]

Figure 4-2 shows Hibbs's data for the 12 countries. The observed association between ideological orientation of the

---

shines impartially on the just and on the unjust," wrote Van Wyck Brooks, "that once you have a point of view all history will back you up." The difficulties in developing generalizations are suggested by Hansen's findings that the important factors shaping U.S. tax policy appear to be unified party control of the presidency and Congress and the changes wrought by realigning elections. See Susan B. Hansen, "Partisan Realignment and Tax Policy, 1789-1970," paper delivered at the annual meeting of the American Political Science Association, September 1977.

[24] Hibbs, "Political Parties and Macroeconomic Policy," p. 1482. The monetary policy of the Federal Reserve Board (measured by fluctuations in the discount rate) does not appear to be responsive to the priorities of the party controlling the White House. This single result does not mean that left-right differences are generally unimportant, as Cowart and Blum seem to conclude. See Andrew T. Cowart and Anthony G. Blum, "Monetary Policy in America: Findings and Some Comparisons with the European Experience," paper presented at the annual meeting of the American Political Science Association, September 1977.

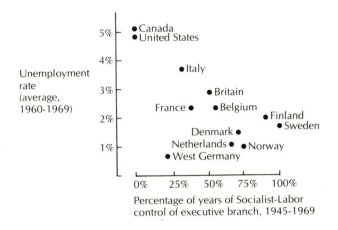

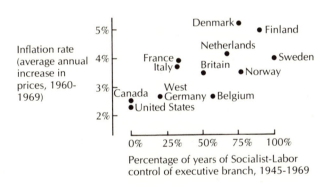

FIGURE 4-2
UNEMPLOYMENT AND INFLATION RATES IN RELATION TO
LENGTH OF EXECUTIVE CONTROL BY SOCIALIST-LABOR
PARTIES (HIBBS'S DATA)

governing political parties and macroeconomic outcomes has the following approximate quantitative character:

—Each additional 10 years of a Socialist government (compared to a Centrist or Conservative government) meant a reduction in the unemployment rate of about 1.7 percent.

—Each additional 10 years of a Socialist government (compared to a Centrist or Conservative government) meant an increase in the inflation rate of about 0.8 percent.

—Differences in the ideological location of the governing political party accounted for about half of the variation in country-to-country differences in inflation and unemployment rates in the 25 years following World War II.[25]

Income equalization in 10 countries. The Left and the Right divide most sharply over the issue of income redistribution. In the survey of party stands of economic objectives

[25] As is evident in the scatterplots, these findings depend mainly on the substantial political and economic differences between the Scandinavian countries (with left-wing governments and greater sensitivity to unemployment and distribution issues) and the United States and Canada (with more centrist governments more preoccupied with inflation). The comparison between the U.S. and Sweden is investigated in the valuable study of Andrew Martin, *The Politics of Economic Policy in the United States: A Tentative View from a Comparative Perspective* (Beverly Hills, Calif.: Sage Publishing, 1973). *Within* countries, the differences in macroeconomic performance due to party politics are more difficult to assess, in part because of time-series problems and the long-run dominance of the Left or the Right in the country. Hibbs did find, however, that (1) in the U.K., Labour (when governing) did better than the Conservatives by 0.6 percent in the unemployment rate and (2) the Democrats did better than the Republicans by 2.4 percent. Finally, as Assar Lindbeck has pointed out to me, it is important to take into account the *initial conditions* faced by each party when it takes office. The Right may appear always to be battling inflation because it inherits a high inflation—low unemployment economy from a defeated government of the Left. Similarly, the Left may inherit high unemployment and low inflation. Some good examples, as well as some good counterexamples, are apparent in postwar economic history.

by Kirschen and his colleagues, Socialist and Conservative parties differed most in their ranking of economic priorities on the issue of "improvement in income distribution," which was recorded as a "dominant objective" for the Left and a "negligible objective" for the Right.[26] Does this divergence in economic priorities result in a divergence in policies and in distributional outcomes between countries governed more often by the Left and countries more often governed by the Right?

While data on income distribution are thin and notoriously vulnerable to problems of definition and measurement assumptions (especially in making comparisons across countries), some new and useful numbers describing the distribution of income before and after taxes have recently been compiled for 10 industrialized democracies.[27] It is thus possible to measure the income equalization induced by tax policy and tax administration, matters which the governing political party can often substantially influence. Table 4-6

TABLE 4-6

PRE-TAX AND POST-TAX DISTRIBUTION OF INCOME,
HIGHEST FIFTH OF HOUSEHOLDS

	Pre-tax share of top 20%	Post-tax share of top 20%	Difference
Australia	38.9%	38.8%	0.1
Canada	43.3%	41.0%	2.3
France	47.0%	46.9%	0.1
Germany	46.8%	46.1%	0.7
Japan	42.5%	41.0%	1.5
Netherlands	45.8%	42.9%	2.9
Norway	40.9%	37.3%	3.6
Sweden	40.5%	37.0%	3.5
United Kingdom	40.3%	38.7%	1.6
United States	44.8%	42.9%	1.9

[26] Kirschen et al., *Economic Policy in Our Time*, 1: 227.

[27] Malcolm Sawyer, "Income Distribution in OECD Countries," *OECD Economic Outlook: Occasional Studies* (July 1976), 3-36.

shows the pre-tax and post-tax share of income received by the 20 percent of households receiving the largest family income for each of the 10 countries. The share of pre-tax income received by the top fifth of households ranged from 38.9 percent in Australia to 47.0 percent in France.

The different tax systems operate on the income distribution in quite different ways in the 10 countries. The difference between pre- and post-tax income shares for the most prosperous fifth is greatest in Norway and Sweden. Income equalization induced by the direct tax system is lowest in Australia and France.

How the tax system performs in redistributing income is a function of the politics of the country. Figure 4-3 shows

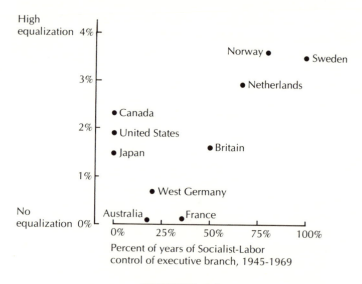

FIGURE 4-3
INCOME REDISTRIBUTION THROUGH DIRECT TAXATION IN
RELATION TO LENGTH OF EXECUTIVE CONTROL
BY SOCIALIST-LABOR PARTIES

the relationship between the degree of income equalization (measured by the difference between pre-tax and post-tax income for the top 20 percent of households) and the extent of left-wing control of the executive branch. In these 10 democracies, income equalization resulting from direct taxes is greatest in countries where the Left has governed the longest.[28]

Size of government budget in 13 countries. Parties of the Left have traditionally favored a more powerful central government than parties of the Right. Governing political parties have translated these preferences into policy. Figure 4-4 shows the very strong relationship between government receipts (as a percent of GNP) and the extent of Socialist-Labor control of the executive in 13 countries. From 1945 to 1969, each additional decade of left-wing control meant an additional 10 percentage point increase in government receipts.[29]

Rate of expansion of public economy in 17 countries.[30] David Cameron has analyzed the relationship between the growth of the public sector, defined as increase from 1960 to 1974 in the ratio

$$\frac{\text{all revenues of all levels of government,}}{\text{gross domestic product}}$$

[28] These conclusions agree with those in Cameron's much more elaborate study of various explanations of cross-national differences in economic inequality. David R. Cameron, "Politics, Public Policy, and Economic Inequality: A Comparative Analysis," paper delivered at the annual meeting of the American Political Science Association, September 1976.

[29] Data on government receipts are from *The OECD Observer*, February 1974.

[30] David R. Cameron, "Open Economies, Electoral Politics, and the Expansion of the Public Economy: A Comparative Analysis," manuscript, 1977. Other recent and helpful reports on the politics of economic management include Rudolf Klein, "The Politics of

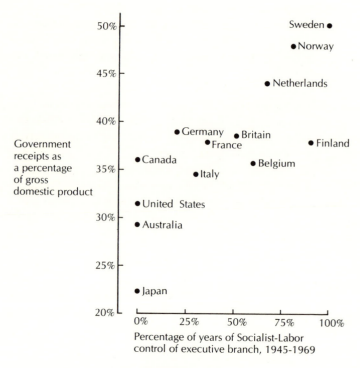

FIGURE 4-4
GOVERNMENT RECEIPTS (AS A PERCENTAGE OF GROSS
DOMESTIC PRODUCT IN 1971-1972) IN RELATION TO
LENGTH OF EXECUTIVE CONTROL BY SOCIALIST-
LABOR PARTIES

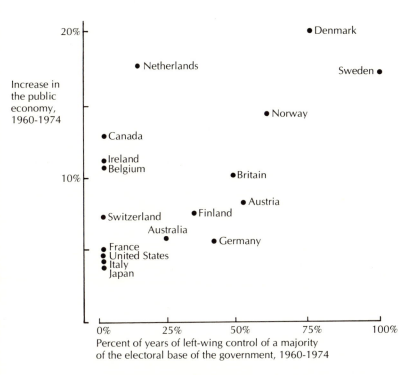

FIGURE 4-5

PARTISANSHIP OF THE GOVERNMENT AND EXPANSION OF
THE PUBLIC ECONOMY, 1960-1974 (CAMERON'S DATA)

and the proportion of the 1960-1974 period that leftist political parties held a majority of the government's electoral base. Figure 4-5 shows the relationship: the longer the control by the Left, the greater the expansion of the public sector.

INTERACTION BETWEEN ELECTORAL CYCLE AND PARTISAN ECONOMIC POLICY

The substantive content and the timing of high-level macroeconomic policy are influenced by at least three factors: the state of the economy itself ("objective" economic conditions); the political-economic ideology of the governing political party; and the electoral-calendar. Obviously these influences are intertwined. The evidence shows:

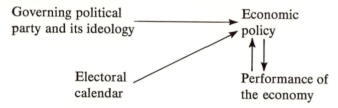

In countries where the governing party can, within a limited span, choose the date of national elections, even the electoral calendar is not exogenous. Flexible electoral calendars, in

Public Expenditure: American Theory and British Practice," *British Journal of Political Science*, 6 (1976), 401-443; and the important work of Andrew T. Cowart, "The Economic Policies of European Governments: Part 1, Monetary Policy," paper delivered at the annual meeting of the American Political Science Association, September 1976. Cowart concludes (p. 41): "Governments of the Left appear to have taken more dramatic action in responding to domestic economic change—whether for the purposes of maximizing the goal of full employment or minimizing price instability. They typically respond in significant ways to unemployment; their response to price instability is non-trivial; and they do not appear hesitant to change monetary policy instruments. . . . The response of governments of the right in the systems is simply more muted in most cases."

addition, affect the performance of the economy through the international electoral-economic cycle:

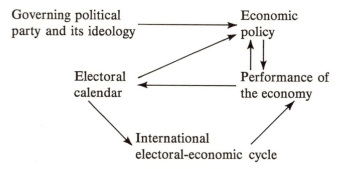

How might those politicians making economic policy weigh the considerations of objective economic conditions, their party's platform, and the electoral calendar? These different forces need not always conflict with one another; the policies advocated in the platform may simply reinforce the policies needed to induce pre-election prosperity—or at least be perceived by incumbents as reinforcing such policies. That is, incumbents may believe that the platform itself contains the plans that will lead to economic prosperity and therefore a good chance of re-election, and so they seek to deliver on platform priorities in time for the election. The incumbents' belief in the platform is enhanced by the fact that it was a winning platform for them in the prior election.

Economic policy-makers must also respond to economic realities. When an economic problem reaches a crisis level— that is, when it reduces the incumbents' probability of being re-elected—then that problem will move to the top of the policy agenda, regardless of party platform priorities.

The combination of crisis and platform decides short-run, pre-election economic policy. Incumbents appear to follow two rules here:

Rule 1: If there is a single, highly visible economic problem that is very important to the electorate, seek pre-election improvements on that problem regardless of the economic priorities of the party platform.

101

It is electorally necessary for the administration to make progress or appear to make progress on any type of major economic problem (if there is one)—whether it be high unemployment or high inflation or an unfavorable balance of payments—before the election. In pre-election economic planning, the crisis area of economic policy dominates the priorities sought by the party platform of the incumbent administration. In 1947, for example, the unemployment rate was 3.6 percent and the inflation rate was 13.1 percent; and clearly, in preparation for the upcoming election, the 1948 economic policies of the incumbent Democrats were unusually sensitive to the problem of inflation.

If there is no specific economic crisis, then a second rule, for "normal times," comes into play:

Rule 2: If no single economic problem is dominant, seek to improve the pre-election economy in the direction of party platform priorities.

For example, if both inflation and unemployment are under reasonable control, a governing party of the Left will seek to improve its electoral chances with pre-election reductions in unemployment at the risk of higher inflation; a governing party of the Right, in contrast, will seek pre-election improvements by attacking inflation.

The pre-election path of unemployment and inflation moved in accordance with these two rules in seven of the eight U.S. presidential elections from 1948 to 1976 (Figure 4-6). Given their very high inflation rates, three of the pre-election periods (1947, 1951, and 1975) fall under Rule 1. Under such conditions, the incumbent administration—Democrats and Republicans alike—succeeded in very substantially reducing the rate of inflation in time for the presidential election. The remaining five presidential elections took place in calmer economic times, when Rule 2 is supposed to hold. In four of five elections, Rule 2 is confirmed. During 1963-1964 and 1967-1968, the Democratic administrations were more successful in reducing unemployment than in reducing inflation. During 1959-1960 and 1971-1972, the Republican

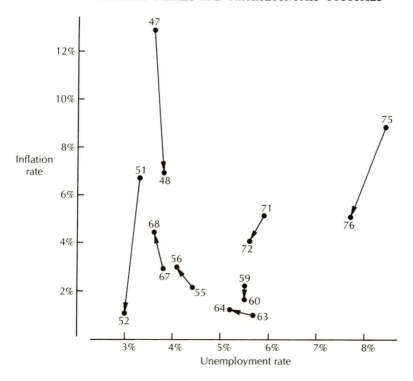

FIGURE 4-6
UNEMPLOYMENT AND INFLATION RATES IN RELATION TO
PRESIDENTIAL ELECTIONS, 1947-1976

incumbents did better on inflation than unemployment. The exception is the 1955-1956 period with its reduction in unemployment and increase in inflation, a Democratic-style outcome under a Republican administration.[31]

(More elaborate and fanciful models describing the joint movements of unemployment and inflation can be based on Rules 1 and 2, particularly when one recalls that interna-

[31] The pattern described here (and in Figure 4-5) is special to the pre-election period. See Table 1-2 for evidence that the inflation-unemployment path during presidential election years differs from the path in other years.

103

tional economic movements may become synchronized and reinforcing as a number of countries start riding the same electoral-economic cycle.[32] One particularly interesting prediction is that the joint path of inflation and unemployment will describe clockwise loops over the electoral cycle under a left-wing government and counterclockwise loops under a right-wing government. The optimum economic point—toward the southwest corner of the inflation-unemployment scatterplot—is of course reached in election years. It is apparent that with all these political variables available to work in combination with all the measures of macroeconomic outcomes, rich possibilities for specification of further models develop.)

CONCLUSION

The single most important determinant of variations in macroeconomic performance from one industrialized democracy to another is the location on the left-right spectrum of the governing political party. Party platforms and political ideology set priorities and help decide policy. The consequence is that the governing political party is very much responsible for major macroeconomic outcomes—unemployment rates, inflation rates, income equalization, and the size and rate of expansion of the government budget.

The electorate, by choosing the governing political party, influences the choice of macroeconomic priorities, at least within the range of options offered by the competitive parties. In addition, if the politicians' theory that voters reward prosperity and punish recession is correct, the electorate makes a judgment about the short-run competence of the governing party's management of the economy. It is now time to find out if voters do in fact reward the governing party for pre-election prosperity.

[32] The only work on this issue is Assar Lindbeck, "Business Cycles, Politics and International Economic Dependence," *Skandinaviska Enskilda Banken Quarterly Review*, 2 (1975), 53-68.

5
Economic and Political Determinants of Electoral Outcomes

The politicians' belief that the level and character of national economic performance significantly determine how voters cast their ballots is the underlying cause of both the electoral-economic cycle and the partisan control of economic policy. The fact of political competition combined with the politicians' view of what it takes to win explains how economic outcomes are shaped and manipulated by the party controlling the government.

Is the politicians' economic model of elections correct? At the extreme, the devastation of the governing party's electoral base in times of economic collapse confirms the view that voters do not like depression and take it out on the incumbents. Chapter 1 showed, however, that many politicians believe that voters respond even to relatively small shifts in economic conditions right before the election—an October dip in employment, a summertime "lull," and the like. Furthermore, the pre-election economic tactics of some incumbent governments, producing finely timed increases in real disposable income, reflect the political assessment that the electorate as a whole possesses a steep economic-dose–political-response curve.

How the electorate responds to varying degrees of prosperity and recession is, of course, an empirical matter.[1] This chapter presents several simple models of U.S. national elections from 1946 to 1976 (presidential as well as on-year and midterm congressional elections) that test whether short-run

[1] See Anthony Downs, *An Economic Theory of Democracy* (New York: Harper and Row, 1957) and Gerald H. Kramer, "Short-Term Fluctuations in U.S. Voting Behavior, 1896-1964," *American Political Science Review*, 65 (March 1971), 131-143.

changes in economic conditions affect the aggregate electoral support won by the candidates of the incumbent party. The resulting data analysis measures the degree to which overall election outcomes represent a referendum on the incumbent administration's handling of the economy and of other issues. Let us begin with a set of elections for which referendum models have often been rejected.

MIDTERM CONGRESSIONAL ELECTIONS

Outcomes of midterm elections appear as a mixture of the routine and the inexplicable. In every off-year congressional election but one since the Civil War, the political party of the incumbent president has lost seats in the House of Representatives, falling back from its gains won in the presidential election two years before. V. O. Key suggested that midterm ballots were not produced by an electorate responding in any consistent fashion to economic or any other measurable factors:

> Since the electorate cannot change administrations at midterm elections, it can only express its approval or disapproval by returning or withdrawing legislative majorities. At least such would be the rational hypothesis about what the electorate might do. In fact, no such logical explanation can completely describe what it does at midterm elections. The Founding Fathers, by the provision for midterm elections, built into the constitutional system a procedure whose strange consequences lack explanation in any theory that personifies the electorate as a rational god of vengeance and of reward.[2]

The diagnosis of midterms as non-elections, as non-referendums, and as merely the routine swing of the electoral pendulum against the in-party became the standard textbook wisdom, as well as an example of something that political

[2] V. O. Key, Jr., *Politics, Parties, and Pressure Groups*, 5th ed. (New York: Thomas Y. Crowell, 1964), pp. 567-568.

scientists knew and professional politicians did not.[3] Many politicians and journalists read the midterm vote as the electorate's evaluation of how well the incumbent administration had done during the two years since its inauguration.[4]

More recently students of politics have come to agree with the politicians' view of midterms as referenda. Kramer reported in his 1971 paper that short-run changes in economic conditions accounted for about 60 percent of the variance in the ups and downs of the national vote; the electorate was more likely to favor the party of the incumbent president in congressional elections when economic times were good in the year before the election and to move toward the out-party in less prosperous times.[5] Then the reality of the 1974 mid-

---

[3] Angus Campbell, "Voters and Elections: Past and Present," *Journal of Politics*, 26 (November 1964), 745-757; Angus Campbell, "Surge and Decline: A Study of Electoral Change," *Public Opinion Quarterly*, 24 (Fall 1960), 397-418; and Key, *Politics, Parties, and Pressure Groups*, pp. 568-569.

[4] Sam Kernell, "Presidential Popularity and Negative Voting: An Alternative Explanation of the Mid-Term Congressional Decline of the President's Party," *American Political Science Review*, 71 (March 1977), 44-66.

[5] Gerald H. Kramer, "Short-Term Fluctuations in U.S. Voting Behavior, 1896-1964." A data error in this paper is corrected in its Bobbs-Merrill reprint (PS-498); see also Saul Goodman and Gerald H. Kramer, "Commentary on Arcelus and Meltzer: The Effect of Aggregate Economic Conditions on Congressional Elections," *American Political Science Review*, 69 (December 1975), 1255-1265. Other studies dealing with the effects of aggregate economic conditions on the national vote are reviewed in Edward R. Tufte, "On the Distribution of Published R^2: Consequences of Selection of Models and Evidence," manuscript, 1977. The recent work includes Franciso Arcelus and Allan H. Meltzer, "The Effect of Aggregate Economic Variables on Congressional Elections," *American Political Science Review*, 69 (December 1975), 1232-1239; Howard S. Bloom and H. Douglas Price, "Voter Response to Short-Run Economic Conditions: The Asymmetric Effect of Prosperity and Recession," *American Political Science Review*, 69 (December 1975), 1240-1254; Ray C. Fair, "On Controlling the Economy to Win Elections," Cowles Foundation Discussion Paper No. 397, Yale University, August 15, 1975; Ray C. Fair, "The Effect of Economic Events on Votes for President," Cowles Foundation Paper No. 418, Yale University,

term congressional election, so clearly a negative referendum on the Republican presidency and the slumping economy, made difficult the continued maintenance of the textbook interpretation.

I will consider the contributions of three factors determining the partisan division of the national congressional vote:

Short-run economic performance under the incumbents   Incumbent advantage or disadvantage on non-economic issues   Long-run strength of the incumbent political party (their "normal" vote")

Votes in national elections, incumbents vs. non-incumbents

The *incumbent party* is taken as the party of the president rather than as the party controlling the House. Since no other targets other than local ones present themselves in off-year elections, it is reasonable to expect that voters upset by the performance of the president will take their dissatisfaction

January 19, 1976; Gerald H. Kramer and Susan J. Lepper, "Congressional Elections," in *The Dimensions of Quantitative Research in History*, ed. William O. Aydelotte, Allan G. Bogue, and Robert William Fogel (Princeton: Princeton University Press, 1972), pp. 256-284; Susan J. Lepper, "Voting Behavior and Aggregate Policy Targets," *Public Choice*, 18 (Summer 1974), 67-81; Allan H. Meltzer and Marc Vellrath, "The Effects of Economic Policies on Votes for the Presidency: Some Evidence from Recent Elections," *Journal of Law and Economics*, 18 (December 1975), 781-798; George J. Stigler, "General Economic Conditions and National Elections," *American Economic Review*, 63 (May 1973), 160-167; and Edward R. Tufte, "Determinants of the Outcomes of Midterm Congressional Elections," *American Political Science Review*, 69 (September 1975), 812-826. For France, see Jean-Jacques Rosa and Daniel Amson, "Conditions Économiques et Élections," *Revue Française de Science Politique*, 26 (December 1976), 1101-1124.

out on the congressional candidates of the president's party.[6] Arseneau and Wolfinger found evidence that "the public image of Congress is rather undifferentiated and, moreover, assessments of the two parties' performance are likely to be determined predominantly by evaluation of the president rather than Congress . . . congressional candidates are likely to suffer or benefit from voters' estimates of how well the president has been doing his job."[7]

The measure of *short-run economic conditions* will be the election-year change in real disposable income per capita (ΔE in the notation of Chapter 1). Since it is "real"—that is, in constant dollars—inflation is discounted. And since it is "disposable," ΔE represents the election-year change in after-tax income.

The measure of the *public's evaluation of incumbent performance on non-economic issues* for midterm elections will be the standard Gallup Poll question: "Do you approve or disapprove of the way President ——— is handling his job as president?"[8]

[6] Cf. Donald E. Stokes and Warren E. Miller, "Party Government and the Saliency of Congress," *Public Opinion Quarterly*, 26 (Winter 1962), 531-546.

[7] Robert B. Arseneau and Raymond E. Wolfinger, "Voting Behavior in Congressional Elections," paper delivered at the annual meeting of the American Political Science Association, September 1973. Further evidence is reported in James E. Piereson, "Presidential Popularity and Midterm Voting at Different Electoral Levels," *American Journal of Political Science*, 19 (November 1975), 683-694; and Kernell, "Presidential Popularity."

[8] The approval rating itself is slightly contaminated with perceptions of how well the economy is performing. Most studies have found a weak-to-moderate relationship between approval ratings and economic conditions. It appears, however, that in times when economic issues become increasingly salient to the electorate, the approval ratings become more closely connected to short-term economic fluctuations. Normally the approval ratings bounce around month by month in response to non-economic events, particularly foreign policy issues, which move so much more quickly—in the headlines at least—than the relatively glacial pace of the national economy. The yearly drift in the ratings, however, is likely to be affected by the course of the economy. Stimson's findings that the ratings are high at the begin-

The measure of the *outcome of the election* will be the share of the nationwide vote won by congressional candidates of the president's party relative to the long-run strength of that party. The long-run, average strength of the incumbent party is taken as the average of the vote that the party has won over the eight preceding elections. This standardization (measuring how each election deviates from a long-run average) is important in the case of congressional elections mainly because of the persistent Democratic advantage. For if the incumbent president is a Democrat and his party receives, say, 52 percent of the vote, that is a relative defeat since the Democrats usually win about 54 percent of the nationwide congressional vote. On the other hand, 52 percent of the congressional vote for the Republicans would be a spectacular victory.

Table 5-1 shows the data for elections from 1946 to 1974. In equation form, the referendum model of midterm outcomes is:

$$\begin{array}{l}\text{Standardized vote} \\ \text{loss by} \\ \text{president's} \\ \text{party in the midterm}\end{array} = \beta_0 + \beta_1 \begin{array}{l}\text{Yearly} \\ \text{change in} \\ \text{economic} \\ \text{conditions}\end{array} + \beta_2 \begin{array}{l}\text{Presidential} \\ \text{popularity}\end{array}$$

The idea is that the lower the approval rating of the incumbent president and the less prosperous the economy, the greater the loss of support for the president's party. Table 5-2 shows the multiple regression estimating the model's coefficients. The fitted equation indicates that:

—A change of one percentage point in the growth of real disposable income per capita in the year before the elec-

---

ning and at the end of the presidential term might be explained by the election-inspired upswings of the economy that occur near the end of the four-year term and spill over to the beginning of the next. See James A. Stimson, "Public Support for American Presidents: A Cyclical Model," *Public Opinion Quarterly*, 40 (Spring 1976), 1-21. In contrast, see Bruno S. Frey and Friedrich Schneider, "Economic and Personality Determinants of Presidential Popularity," manuscript, 1977.

TABLE 5-1
MIDTERM ELECTIONS, 1946-1974

Year	V_t Nationwide midterm congressional vote for party of incumbent president	N_t^8 Mean congressional vote for party of incumbent president in 8 prior elections	$Y_t = V_t - N_t^8$ Standardized vote loss (−) or gain (+) by president's party in midterm election	P_t Gallup Poll rating of president at time of election	ΔE_t Yearly change in real disposable income per capita
1946	45.27%	Democratic 52.57%	−7.30%	32%	−2.6%
1950	50.04%	Democratic 52.04%	−2.00%	43%	5.9%
1954	47.27%	Republican 49.77%	−2.50%	65%	−0.6%
1958	43.60%	Republican 49.75%	−6.15%	56%	−0.5%
1962	52.64%	Democratic 51.75%	0.89%	67%	2.6%
1966	51.33%	Democratic 53.20%	−1.87%	48%	3.9%
1970	45.77%	Republican 46.54%	−0.77%	56%	3.0%
1974	41.38%	Republican 46.17%	−4.51%	55%	−2.3%
1978		Democratic 54.40%			

TABLE 5-2

MIDTERM CONGRESSIONAL ELECTIONS:
MULTIPLE REGRESSION

$$Y_i = \beta_0 + \beta_1(\Delta E_i) + \beta_2 P_i + u_i$$

	Regression coefficient and standard error	Simple correlation with midterm loss
Yearly change in real disposable income per capita (ΔE)	$\hat{\beta}_1 = .622$ .166	.72
Presidential approval rating (P)	$\hat{\beta}_2 = .132$ .044	.58
$\hat{\beta}_0 = -10.74$		
$R^2 = 0.825$		

tion is associated with a national change of 0.6 percentage points in the midterm vote for the congressional candidates of the president's party (Figure 5-1).

—A change in presidential popularity of 10 percentage points in the Gallup Poll is associated with a national change of 1.3 percentage points in the national midterm vote for congressional candidates of the president's party.

The model fits well and the observed effects are strong.[9] A year of prosperous growth (say a 3.0 percent increase in real disposable income) compared to a mild recession (a decline of 1.0 percent) is worth an extra 2.5 percent of the vote, which would typically translate into an extra 20 to 30 seats in the House of Representatives. That is about the same as the difference between having a presidential approval rat-

[9] Two-thirds of the residual sum of squares comes from the 1958 election, when the Democrats won 56.4 percent of the vote despite the model's prediction of 53.9 percent.

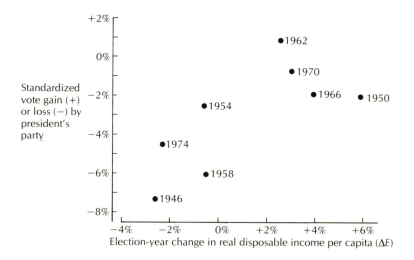

FIGURE 5-1

ELECTION-YEAR ECONOMIC PERFORMANCE AND THE VOTE
IN MIDTERM CONGRESSIONAL ELECTIONS

ing of 60 percent and 40 percent. In midterm elections, the
party of a popular president in prosperous times will win
from 40 to 60 congressional seats more than the party of an
unpopular president in times of economic recession.

These estimates of the electoral effect of changes in real
disposable income growth and presidential approval rating
help us to assess the impact of each factor in the 1974 midterm. When President Ford came into office in August 1974,
Republican chances increased substantially. Ford's approval
rating was initially 71 percent; Nixon's had been running in
the low twenties in the months before he resigned. This 50
percent shift in presidential approval translated, according
to the model, into about 6 percent of the national congressional vote. Then came the pardon of Nixon, and Ford's

113

rating fell 20 points, costing the Republicans about 2.5 percent of the congressional vote. The economic decline of 1974 played an even more important role in creating the Democratic surge. During that election year, real disposable income per capita dropped by 2.3 percent. Compared to the 1970 midterm year, when real disposable income had increased by 3.0 percent per capita, the 1974 economic dropoff cost Republican congressional candidates about 5 percent of the vote.

Survey interviews conducted during the 1974 campaign confirm the interpretations based on the aggregate model. The Democratic vote ran 11 percentage points higher than normal among those who thought the government was doing a poor job on economic policy, whereas those who liked government efforts at economic management voted only one percent more Democratic than normal. For a majority of voters, economic issues influenced their decision more than the remains of Watergate.[10]

An equation forecasting the 1978 midterm results from solving the fitted equation of Table 5-2 and substituting in the normal Democratic vote (N^8 for 1978 is 54.40 percent):

Nationwide congressional
vote for Democrats $= 43.66 + .622(\Delta E) + .132(P)$,
in 1978 midterm election

where ΔE is the percentage change in real disposable income per capita over the 12 months right before the election and P is the president's approval rating (in the Gallup Poll) in September-October 1978. Both P and ΔE are known in advance of the election. For previous midterms, the forecasts from the model have been as accurate as pre-election polls predicting vote. Over a range of values of P and ΔE, the predicted 1978 Democratic congressional vote is:

[10] *ISR Newsletter*, Institute for Social Research, University of Michigan (Summer 1976), 6-7; and Arthur H. Miller and Richard Glass, "Economic Dissatisfaction and Electoral Choice," manuscript, 1976.

	Change in real disposable income per capita		
	0%	+2%	+4%
Gallup Poll approval rating — 40%	48.9%	50.2%	51.4%
50%	50.3%	51.5%	52.8%
60%	51.6%	52.8%	54.1%

Since the Democrats won 57.3 percent of the congressional vote in 1976, it is likely that they will lose at least several percentage points of that vote in 1978, unless the economy is booming (a gain in ΔE of around 6 percent) and the president's approval rating equals past highs (65 to 70 percent).

The vote cast in midterm congressional elections, then, is a referendum on the performance of the president and his administration's management of the economy. Although the in-party's share of the vote almost invariably declines in the midterm compared to the previous on-year election, the magnitude of that loss is substantially smaller if the president has a high level of popular approval, if the economy is performing well, or both.[11]

ON-YEAR CONGRESSIONAL ELECTIONS

What with the electoral-economic cycle, the years of presidential elections are usually quite prosperous. From 1948 to 1976 that election-year prosperity varied somewhat in degree, ranging from a minimum of no change at all in real disposable income per capita in 1960 to a maximum increase of 5.6 percent in 1964. Do these differing degrees of prosperity account for the extent of electoral support won by members of the incumbent party in the on-year congressional elections?

[11] The midterm model is developed in additional substantive and technical detail in my *Data Analysis for Politics and Policy* (Englewood Cliffs, N.J.: Prentice-Hall, 1974), pp. 139-146, and "Determinants of the Outcomes of Midterm Congressional Elections." Those presentations contain further statistical validations of the model. Some slight data errors in the previous versions have been corrected here.

The electoral effect of economic conditions in on-year elections will be assessed with a model similar to that used for midterms. The pre-election shift in real disposable income will be matched up against the shift in the normalized vote for the incumbent party (the party holding the presidency at the time of the election). The potential impact of the presidential candidates on the on-year congressional vote will be measured on the basis of survey interviews conducted during each election, asking citizens what they liked and disliked about the two presidential candidates. During each campaign since 1948, interviews with a national sample of the electorate conducted by the Survey Research Center at the University of Michigan have included a long series of questions asking voters to describe in their own words what they liked and disliked about the candidates:

> I'd like to ask you what you think are the good and bad points about [the two presidential candidates]. Is there anything in particular that you like about [the Democratic presidential candidate]? What is that? . . . Anything else? . . . Anything else? . . . Anything else? . . . Anything else?
>
> Is there anything in particular that you don't like about [the Democratic presidential candidate]? What is that? . . . Anything else? . . . Anything else? . . . Anything else? . . . Anything else?

The same insistent questions were also asked about the Republican candidate. Each respondent could give up to five likes and five dislikes about each candidate, and the replies were then classified into one of six categories: foreign issues, domestic issues, group-related concerns, evaluations of the different parties as managers of government, attitudes toward the Democratic candidate, and attitudes toward the Republican candidate.[12] Responses classified as an "attitude toward

[12] See Donald E. Stokes, Angus Campbell, and Warren E. Miller, "Components of Electoral Decision," *American Political Science Review*, 52 (June 1958), 367-387; Donald E. Stokes, "Some Dynamic

the candidate" included mentions of such matters as the candidate's record and experience, qualifications and abilities, relationship to political party, and personal qualities. From all the interviews in each election-year survey, the average number of favorable and unfavorable mentions for each candidate was computed. The difference of the averaged number of favorable and unfavorable mentions between the Democratic and Republican candidates—the *net candidate advantage*—will be used along with the yearly change in real disposable income to account for the outcomes of on-year congressional elections.[13] The net candidate advantage is the analogue to the presidential approval rating used in the description of midterm elections. Only one national target, the president, is available for voters during the off-year elections, but presidential elections involve comparisons between alternatives, and that is what this measure is supposed to capture. The net candidate advantage is measured relative to the "incumbent," who is defined as the candidate of the party holding the presidency at the time of the election. In 1948, 1956, 1964, 1972, and 1976, the incumbent was simply the president seeking re-election. In the remaining elections, the incumbent candidate is taken as Stevenson in 1952, Nixon in 1960, and Humphrey in 1968. The net candidate advantage is correlated 0.91 with the nationwide presidential vote from 1948 to 1976.

Tables 5-3 and 5-4 show the data and the multiple regression for on-year congressional elections. Once again there is

---

Elements of Contests for the Presidency," *American Political Science Review*, 60 (March 1966), 19-28; and Michael R. Kagay and Greg A. Caldeira, " 'I Like the Looks of His Face': Elements of Electoral Choice, 1952-1972," paper presented at the annual meeting of the American Political Science Association, September 1975.

[13] The net candidate advantage is based on all interview responses dealing with the character or image of the candidates. It equals

$$\left(\begin{array}{cc}\text{favorable} & \text{unfavorable}\\ \text{mentions of} - \text{mentions of}\\ \text{incumbent} & \text{incumbent}\end{array}\right) - \left(\begin{array}{cc}\text{favorable} & \text{unfavorable}\\ \text{mentions of} - \text{mentions of}\\ \text{non-incumbent} & \text{non-incumbent}\end{array}\right)$$

TABLE 5-3

ON-YEAR CONGRESSIONAL ELECTIONS, 1948-1976

Year	V_i Nationwide congressional vote for party of incumbent president	N_i^8 Mean congressional vote for party of incumbent president in 8 prior elections	$Y_i = V_i - N_i^8$ Standardized vote loss (−) or gain (+) by president's party	ΔE_i Yearly change in real disposable income per capita	C_i Net presidential candidate advantage (if $C_i > 0$, incumbent has advantage; if $C_i < 0$, non-incumbent has advantage)
1948	53.24%	Democratic 52.50%	+0.75%	3.4%	+0.093
1952	50.15%	Democratic 51.27%	−1.12%	1.1%	−0.408
1956	48.80%	Republican 49.53%	−0.73%	2.6%	+1.146
1960	45.03%	Republican 48.66%	−3.63%	0.0%	+0.367
1964	57.50%	Democratic 52.67%	+4.83%	5.6%	+1.044
1968	50.92%	Democratic 53.37%	−2.45%	2.8%	−0.353
1972	47.34%	Republican 46.35%	+0.99%	3.3%	+0.902
1976	42.74%	Republican 45.89%	−3.15%	3.3%	−0.221

TABLE 5-4

ON-YEAR CONGRESSIONAL ELECTIONS: MULTIPLE REGRESSION

$$Y_i = \beta_0 + \beta_1(\Delta E_i) + \beta_2 C_i + u_i$$

	Regression coefficient and standard error	Simple correlation with on-year vote
Yearly change in real disposable income per capita (ΔE)	$\hat{\beta}_1 = 1.06$ .44	.77
Net presidential candidate advantage, likes/dislikes (C)	$\hat{\beta}_2 = 1.48$ 1.14	.59
$\hat{\beta}_0 = -3.98$		
$R^2 = .702$		

no doubt that pre-election economic conditions—in this case the degree of on-year prosperity—significantly determine national election outcomes. An election-year change of 1.0 percent in real disposable income has typically produced a change of 1.1 percent in the national vote for congressional candidates of the in-party (Figure 5-2). Thus the difference between a mediocre and a buoyant election-year economy has counted for shifts of three or four percentage points in the vote, which translates into an equivalent swing of 25 to 45 House seats.[14] And that is a very big difference.

[14] The rate of translation of votes into seats (the "swing ratio") has decreased in recent decades from about 2.5 to its present value between 1.2 and 1.5. See Edward R. Tufte, "The Relationship Between Seats and Votes in Two-Party Systems," *American Political Science Review*, 67 (June 1973), 540-554; and Edward R. Tufte, "Communication," *American Political Science Review*, 68 (March 1974), 211-213.

119

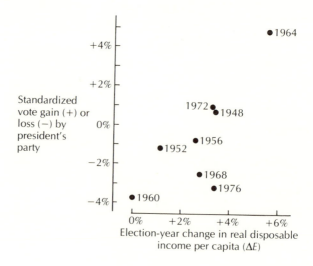

FIGURE 5-2

ELECTION-YEAR ECONOMIC PERFORMANCE AND THE VOTE
IN ON-YEAR CONGRESSIONAL ELECTIONS

PRESIDENTIAL ELECTIONS[15]

The usual model

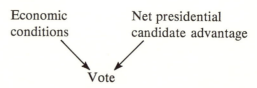

will be used to assess the effect of economic fluctuations on
the vote for president. For presidential elections, unlike congressional elections, the complication of standardizing the
vote for the long-run dominance by the Democrats does not

[15] This section is co-authored with Jan Juran and draws on Jan
Juran, "Determinants of the Outcomes of Presidential Elections,"
manuscript, 1975.

arise. Although the Republican party has failed to win a majority of seats in either the House or Senate since their victories in the elections of November 1952, Republican presidential candidates have been much more competitive, winning half the contests since 1948 and out-polling Democratic candidates in total votes. Republican presidential contenders received a grand total of 270,289,000 votes from 1948 to 1976, compared with 255,594,000 votes for Democratic contenders. To measure the outcome of the presidential election, therefore, I will use the share of the vote won by the presidential candidate of the incumbent party. Tables 5-5 and 5-6 show the data and analysis.

TABLE 5-5

PRESIDENTIAL ELECTIONS, 1948-1976

Year	"Incumbent" presidential candidate	V_i National vote for incumbent	ΔE_i Yearly change in real disposable income per capita	C_i Net presidential candidate advantage (if $C_i > 0$, incumbent has advantage; if $C_i < 0$, non-incumbent has advantage)
1948	Truman	52.37%	3.4%	+0.093
1952	Stevenson	44.59%	1.1%	−0.408
1956	Eisenhower	57.76%	2.6%	+1.146
1960	Nixon	49.91%	0.0%	+0.367
1964	Johnson	61.34%	5.6%	+1.044
1968	Humphrey	49.59%	2.8%	−0.353
1972	Nixon	61.79%	3.3%	+0.902
1976	Ford	48.89%	3.3%	−0.221

The multiple regression accounts for nearly all the statistical variation in the national vote for president. The substance of the regression coefficients in Table 5-6 is:

—A 1.0 percent improvement in real disposable income per capita benefits the incumbent presidential candidate by 1.3 percent of the national vote (Figure 5-3).

121

TABLE 5-6

PRESIDENTIAL ELECTIONS: MULTIPLE REGRESSION

$$V_t = \beta_0 + \beta_1(\Delta E_t) + \beta_2 C_t + u_t$$

	Regression coefficient and standard error	Simple correlation with presidential vote
Yearly change in real disposable income per capita (ΔE)	$\hat{\beta}_1 = 1.32$ .45	.64
Net presidential candidate advantage, likes/dislikes (C)	$\hat{\beta}_2 = 7.64$ 1.25	.91

$\hat{\beta}_0 = 47.22$
$R^2 = .942$

—Suppose that a voter, upon canvassing his or her likes and dislikes about the character of the two presidential candidates, favors a candidate by one "like"—that is, by one additional favorable mention—over the other candidate. That advantage, if true *on average* for all voters, benefits the favored candidate by 7.6 percentage points over the other candidate.

The economic factor is a very powerful one in presidential elections. The successful election-year stimulation of the economy by incumbents produces a significant advantage that persistently pays off in votes. As the fitted equations show (and as we already knew anyway), short-run economic fluctuations are not singly decisive in presidential elections. Differences in voters' evaluations of the character and competence of the two candidates weigh heavily in the electoral verdict and can overcome an incumbent advantage arising from election-year economic upswings. No doubt the state of the economy affects different elections somewhat differently

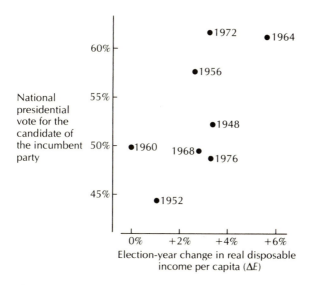

FIGURE 5-3

ELECTION-YEAR ECONOMIC PERFORMANCE AND THE VOTE
IN PRESIDENTIAL ELECTIONS

—depending upon the particular mix of economic conditions, the salience of economic issues in relation to other issues in the campaign, and the dozens of idiosyncratic influences unique to each presidential campaign. Despite all the short-run "noise" in presidential contests, the extent of prosperity prevailing in the election year remains a regular and significant determinant of the vote won by the nominee of the in-party.

COATTAIL EFFECTS AND ECONOMIC CONDITIONS
IN ON-YEAR ELECTIONS

The electoral fortunes of the presidential candidate of the incumbent party and those members of Congress belonging

123

to the incumbent party tend to move together.[16] The standardized on-year congressional vote and the presidential vote share 53 percent of their statistical variation:

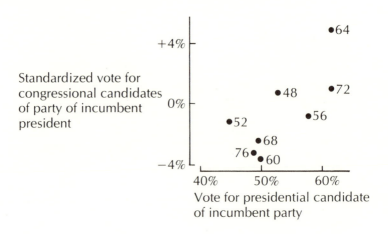

On-year presidential and congressional elections have much in common, because the same factors—economic conditions and net candidate advantage—determine the outcomes of

[16] On the unsettled matter of coattail effects, see Warren E. Miller, "Presidential Coattails: A Study in Political Myth and Methodology," *Public Opinion Quarterly*, 19 (Winter 1955-1956), 353-368; Angus Campbell and Warren E. Miller, "The Motivational Basis of Straight and Split Ticket Voting," *American Political Science Review*, 51 (June 1957), 293-312; Milton C. Cummings, Jr., *Congressmen and the Electorate* (New York: Free Press, 1966), which is the most detailed study; Robert A. Schoenberger, "Campaign Strategy and Party Loyalty: The Electoral Relevance of Candidate Decision-Making in the 1964 Congressional Elections," *American Political Science Review*, 63 (June 1969), 515-520; and Gary C. Jacobson, "Presidential Coattails in 1972," *Public Opinion Quarterly*, 40 (1976), 194-200; Richard P. Y. Li, "A Dynamic Comparative Analysis of Presidential and House Elections," *American Journal of Political Science*, 20 (November 1976), 671-691.

both. For the presidential and on-year congressional elections from 1948 to 1976, the correlations are:

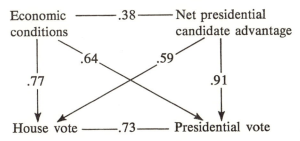

The correlations (and a separate analysis regressing out the effects of ΔE and C from the vote) indicate that congressional and on-year congressional elections tend to shift together for two reasons: (1) the common influence of short-run economic conditions on both elections, and (2) coattail effects, as the top of the ticket influences votes in congressional races. Both these elements appear to operate at roughly equal strength—and so about half of what appears as a coattail effect results merely from the fact that both elections take place in the same economic climate.

DO ONLY BAD TIMES MATTER?

A variation on the theme that good times benefit incumbents and bad times the out-party is that "a party already in power is rewarded much less for good times than it is punished for bad times."[17] Certainly the punishment for very

[17] Angus Campbell, Philip E. Converse, Warren E. Miller, and Donald E. Stokes, *The American Voter* (New York: John Wiley, 1960), p. 555. Similarly, "an incumbent American president has more to fear from an economic recession at election time than from any other condition. There is ample evidence that the 'ins' suffer from recession whether they are demonstrably responsible or not" (Murray Edelman, *The Symbolic Uses of Politics* [Chicago: University of Illinois Press, 1967], p. 82). An empirical study of congressional elections is Bloom and Price, "Voter Response to Short-Run Economic Conditions," 1240-1254.

bad times—such as the Great Depression—was hard and long-lasting for the Republican party. Further, the data for midterm elections from 1946 to 1974 faintly hint that voters may punish more than reward (Figure 5-1). But the hypothesis is not clearly relevant or testable for presidential and on-year congressional elections from 1948 to 1976 because the incumbent party, thanks in part to the electoral-economic cycle, has *always* enjoyed prosperity—of varying degrees to be sure—in presidential election years. As shown in Table 5-5, ΔE has always been positive (if that is what the vague term "good times" means) during on-years. The evidence, furthermore, for on-year elections shows that degrees of prosperity make a great difference in the electoral support won by the incumbent party. Figures 5-2 and 5-3 in particular reveal an electorate rewarding very good economic times considerably more than moderately good times. By the regression estimates, an on-year increase of 4.0 percent in real disposable income yields 2.4 to 3.0 percent more of the vote for incumbents (in both congressional and presidential elections) than a more routine gain of 2.0 percent. Such a difference has historically been worth 15 to 30 congressional seats. Such a difference has exceeded the winning margin in 4 of 8 presidential elections from 1948 to 1976. The degree of prosperity is significant.

Finally, the distinction between "good times" and "bad times" when measured by aggregate data should not be overdrawn. Even when real disposable income per capita increases substantially, many people are still not moving with the economic trend; their real disposable income has not increased. The economic sun does not shine evenly on all voters in good years, nor does rain fall evenly in bad years. For example, when real disposable income increased by an aggregate 3.3 percent in 1976, 28 percent of the voters in an election-day survey reported that their family's financial condition had declined over the year, 50 percent said it had remained the same, and only 22 percent reported improvement. In 1972, when real disposable income also increased by 3.3 percent, 22 percent of the respondents in a survey reported that their economic conditions had worsened over the year, 42 percent said things were the same, and 36 percent felt they were better off.

PERCEIVED CHANGE IN PERSONAL ECONOMIC SITUATION AND THE VOTE: SURVEY DATA

Many different descriptions of the underlying electorate are consistent with electoral outcomes that appear, overall, to be responsive to objective changes in economic conditions. Not every voter responds to every jiggle in real disposable income. Aggregate responsiveness—for which there is good evidence—does not imply a unique specification or characterization of individual voters or groups of voters. Aggregate data describe only the aggregate electoral outcome (which is, of course, what counts in elections). Do more than a few voters actually have economic matters on their minds when they vote? Survey interviews with individual voters conducted during election campaigns will help answer this question.[18]

Table 5-7 shows the relationship between how people saw their financial affairs and their vote for president in 1968, 1972, and 1976.[19] Let us first look at the two Nixon elec-

[18] Such studies include Campbell, Converse, Miller, and Stokes, *The American Voter*, chapter 14; David Butler and Donald Stokes, *Political Change in Britain*, 2nd ed. (New York: St. Martin's Press, 1974), chapter 18; Jeffrey W. Wides, "Self-Perceived Economic Change and Political Orientation," *American Politics Quarterly*, 4 (October 1976), 395-411; Morris Fiorina, "Economic Conditions and American National Elections: A Micro-Analysis," manuscript, 1975; and Miller and Glass, "Economic Dissatisfaction and Electoral Choice."

[19] For 1968 and 1972, the data are from the national surveys conducted by the Survey Research Center at the University of Michigan. The 1976 data are from the NBC election-day survey of voters. The surveys conducted by the Survey Research Center in the elections of 1948 and 1952 do not have a question dealing with recent

127

TABLE 5-7

VOTE FOR PRESIDENT AND FAMILY FINANCIAL SITUATION
OVER PAST YEAR: 1968, 1972, AND 1976

1968 presidential election	*Would you say that you and your family are better off or worse off financially than you were a year ago?*		
	Better	*Same*	*Worse*
Humphrey	54%	47%	35%
Nixon	46	53	65
	100%	100%	100%
N	285	415	161

1972 presidential election	*Would you say that you and your family are better off or worse off financially than you were a year ago?*		
	Better	*Same*	*Worse*
McGovern	31%	30%	48%
Nixon	69	70	52
	100%	100%	100%
N	247	279	153

1976 presidential election	*Compared to a year ago, would you say that your family is financially better off today, about the same, worse off today, or not sure?*		
	Better	*Same*	*Worse*
Carter	30%	51%	77%
Ford	70	49	23
	100%	100%	100%
N	3262	6924	3908

tions. In 1968, as the candidate of the out-party, he won his greatest support from those who saw their personal financial conditions in decline. In 1972, however, as the incumbent, he ran worst among voters who saw their personal financial conditions in decline: same candidate, same party, but different incumbency status.[20] Conversely, Humphrey, as the candidate of the incumbent party in 1968, was most favored by the economically content and least favored by the discontent. In contrast, McGovern did best—running nearly even against Nixon—among those who had had a bad year economically. Not many votes, however, were to be found there, given the booming economy and all the pre-election action in transfer payments in 1972.

Comparable data for the 1976 election are at the bottom of Table 5-7. In 14,000 interviews at the polls on election day, voters were asked to describe their own family's financial path over the year. Those who felt they had become better off preferred Ford over Carter by 40 percentage points; those who felt they had become worse off favored Carter over Ford by 54 percentage points.

Although the connection between the vote and personal economic conditions was very strong in the 1976 election, the data and findings are not as tidy as they initially appear.

---

changes in family financial conditions; those conducted in 1956, 1960, and 1964 used a question with a different time horizon ("During the last few years, has your financial situation been getting better, getting worse, or has it stayed the same?") than in 1968 and 1972. Fiorina, who looked at the survey evidence for the elections from 1952 to 1972, concludes that election returns follow economic conditions "for some elections at some times." In those elections where the link between self-perceived economic conditions (over some time horizon or other) and the vote is weak, the economic issue may have had low salience, or else the net partisan advantage on the economic issue balanced off, even though the issue may have been quite important in that election.

[20] Butler and Stokes, *Political Change in Britain*, pp. 378-392, find a comparable reversal effect in British elections during the 1960s.

The complications begin with the observation that Democrats were much more disappointed about their own financial affairs during 1976 than Republicans: 38 percent of the Democrats said they had slid downhill financially, compared to 14 percent of the Republicans. It was not just that the wealthier Republicans were less affected by the mediocre economy than the poorer Democrats—because, at every income level, nearly three times as many Democrats as Republicans said they had had a bad year. Within each party and income level, the following percentages of people reported that they were worse off financially in 1976:

		Democrats	Republicans
Income	<$5	56%	19%
(thousands	$5-$10	47%	17%
of dollars)	$10-$15	39%	15%
	$15-$25	33%	13%
	>$25	25%	9%

Surely not many Democratic families actually had a worse economic year than Republican families, at least once income level is taken into account. (The differences by income, reading down the columns of the table, probably do reflect the economic realities of 1976, particularly the pressure of widespread unemployment on those with lower incomes.) It appears that selective perception and rationalization affect how voters of different partisan persuasions judge the performance of the national economy, and even what they claim to be their *own family's* state of financial affairs over the year. Would the evaluations of the economy made by members of the parties have differed if there had been a Democratic president and a mediocre economy—that is, would Republicans have been more gloomy than Democrats about the year's financial results? In 1968 the Democrats were the White House incumbents—and sure enough more Republicans reported that financial matters had deteriorated over the year. In 1968, 21 percent of Republican voters compared to

17 percent of Democratic voters said that their families were worse off financially during that year. In 1972, with the Republicans holding the presidency, the Democrats became the pessimists: 24 percent reported worsening of their families' financial affairs compared to 19 percent of the Republicans. In summary, the proportions who reported a worsening of family finances during the year were:

	Democrats	Republicans
1968 (Democratic president)	17%	21%
1972 (Republican president)	24%	19%
1976 (Republican president)	38%	14%

These differences between Democrats and Republicans are maintained within different income levels in each of the three election surveys; the results cannot therefore be explained away by the hypothesis that the class composition of the parties had shifted over the three elections.

(Our findings here have obvious but interesting implications for surveys of consumer confidence used in economic forecasting. Since some people view the economy and even their own personal economic movement through a political filter of their party affiliation and that of the incumbent president and since there are a lot more Democrats than Republicans, it should be the case that consumer confidence and general economic optimism will be greater—even when objective economic conditions are identical—under Democratic than under Republican administrations. Thus the party affiliation of the respondents should be a control variable in measuring consumer economic confidence.)

If the confounding influences of class and party on perceptions of family finances are removed, does there remain a relationship between perceived economic fluctuations and the vote? Table 5-8 provides an answer for the 1976 election by showing the Carter vote in relation to party, income, and direction of change in family financial conditions during 1976. This is an impressive table, especially as survey evi-

TABLE 5-8

CARTER VOTE: BY POLITICAL PARTY, INCOME, AND
FAMILY FINANCIAL CONDITIONS OVER PAST YEAR

		Compared to a year ago, would you say that your family is financially better off today, about the same, worse off today, or not sure?		
Percent for Carter:				
Among Democrats		Better	Same	Worse
	< $5	91%	89%	97%
	$5-$10	63%	87%	95%
Income (000)	$10-$15	72%	84%	95%
	$15-$25	63%	84%	92%
	> $25	71%	83%	92%
Among Republicans		Better	Same	Worse
	< $5	9%	8%	32%
	$5-$10	1%	5%	24%
Income (000)	$10-$15	3%	8%	24%
	$15-$25	3%	7%	20%
	> $25	2%	6%	25%

Percentage bases:

Democrats	32	170	267	Republicans	46	118	38
	62	508	497		121	282	84
	190	728	591		258	445	120
	263	782	520		419	589	150
	231	373	200		403	401	79

dence goes, sorting the 1976 vote into nearly mutually exclusive categories. Carter won less than 3 percent of the votes of Republicans with incomes of more than $5,000 (95 percent of all Republicans) whose perceived financial conditions improved over the year. At the other political-economic extreme, the Carter vote ran about 95 percent among the worse-off Democrats.

The political party identification of the voter had the strongest relation to the vote, accounting for roughly a 70 percentage point swing in support for Carter; the direction of change in family financial conditions accounted for roughly a 20 percentage point swing within the various income and party groups. The effect of income on the vote, although confounded by party and family financial conditions (the wealthy are Republican and more likely to see economic conditions as improving), is apparent: the Ford vote increased across the board as income increased (regardless of party or economic perceptions).[21]

The same factors—party affiliation and perception of how the economy was going—very much affected how citizens evaluated Carter once he became president. In a national survey conducted in late April 1977, the following percent-

---

[21] The evidence presented in this discussion of survey-level data makes a considerably stronger case for the link between economic conditions and the vote than several other studies examining a somewhat wider range of evidence. See, for example, Fiorina, "Economic Conditions and American National Elections." This is in part because of my heavier reliance on recent elections and, particularly, the impressive results found in the 1976 election-day survey. As suggested in n. 19, I have less confidence in the pre-1968 surveys because of the wording of the question dealing with family finances. Clearly there is much analysis left to be done, especially in examining the economic content in the "likes/dislikes" questions on the presidential election surveys. Perhaps those questions will also help assess the relative salience of economic issues in each election. Since the aggregate-level models are models for voters only, the micro-level models probably should be based on interviews with those respondents who claimed that they actually voted.

ages of people reported that they approved Carter's handling of his job as president:

	Percent approving Carter		
	Democrats	Independents	Republicans
Economy seen as			
getting better	89%	75%	61%
staying same	74%	64%	47%
getting worse	63%	47%	45%

Here, then, an economy seen as moving upward (instead of staying the same) was worth an extra 10 to 15 points in the presidential approval rating among Democrats, Independents, and Republicans alike.[22]

In addition to their direct economic effect on the wellbeing of voters, general economic conditions may also influence electoral outcomes through the climate of optimism or pessimism created by the *news* of economic ups and downs.[23] Unfortunately, however, it is difficult to imagine a research design or good evidence that would separate out the effect of the news of economic conditions from how those conditions actually affect people.

[22] From a national telephone survey of 1,707 people conducted in late April 1977 by CBS News and the *New York Times*. These results for President Carter fit very well with the data and interpretations for evaluations of President Ford provided by Miller and Miller, "Partisanship and Performance: 'Rational' Choice in the 1976 Presidential Elections."

[23] Butler and Stokes, *Political Change in Britain*, p. 370, provide a plausible story:

A rise in the unemployment figures has a clear meaning for the ordinary citizen because he can picture its consequences in personal terms and news of such a rise may create a sense of unease in millions of people who themselves are for the moment quite unaffected by it. In a similar way, news of a general price increase can give point to price changes that the voter can recall from recent shopping. Even a national deficit in the balance of payments has some meaning for ordinary people who could not trace the effects that the deficit will have on their own well-being but who know from everyday experience the unpleasant consequences of a deficit in their personal or household accounts.

THE IMPACT OF THE ELECTORAL-ECONOMIC CYCLE ON ELECTION OUTCOMES

How much is the extraordinarily buoyant economy of election years worth to the incumbent party? This question can be answered, approximately to be sure, by combining estimates of how much the electoral-economic cycle affects real disposable income with the estimates of how much real disposable income affects the vote for the incumbent party.

In those years when the incumbent president has sought re-election, ΔE has increased by an average of 3.3 percent. In odd-numbered years, ΔE increased by an average of 1.5 percent. (These data are from Table 1-3.) Let us take the election-year economic advantage to be the difference, or 1.8 percentage points. From Table 5-5, we know that such a change in real disposable income translates into 2.4 percentage points of the national vote for president. Solely because of the electoral-economic cycle, then, the incumbent president has typically started his bid for re-election with a lead of 52.4 percent to 47.6 percent over the candidate of the out-party. That is a very good start, and helps explain why incumbent presidents rarely lose their bid for re-election.

In on-year congressional elections, the electoral-economic cycle benefits the party of the president by an extra 12 to 25 seats in the House of Representatives. In midterm elections, when the electoral-economic cycle is not as powerful as in on-years, the party of the president benefits by approximately 5 to 10 seats—again solely because the economy does better in even-numbered years than in odd-numbered years. Note that a substantial part of the losses suffered by the president's party in midterm congressional elections are the consequence of the weaker economic stimulation in the midterm year compared to the presidential election year two years before. Thus the electoral-economic cycle accounts, to a significant degree, for both coattail effects in presidential elections and for the midterm losses suffered by the president's party.

CONCLUSION: THE POLITICIANS' THEORY CONFIRMED

Outcomes of national elections, taken as a whole, are partially the product of pre-election changes of ordinary magnitude in national economic conditions, taken as a whole. Short-run changes in real disposable income per capita have had a strong effect on the fortunes of the presidential party in midterm congressional elections, on-year congressional elections, and presidential elections since 1948. The effect is a strong and persistent one, statistically secure and politically significant. There is no doubt why politicians have come to believe that short-run economic performance has so much to do with deciding their tenure in office.

By 1971, the politicians' economic theory of election outcomes and the formal statistical assessments of the electoral impact of macroeconomic fluctuations had come full circle— for it was then that high-level economic advisers did their own statistical studies testing the politicians' theory! Gearing up for the 1972 campaign, staff members of the Office of Management and Budget under the direction of the Assistant Director for Evaluation developed statistical models and ran multiple regressions assessing the influence of economic conditions on the outcomes of presidential elections. The OMB studies concluded that between-election increases in real net national product per capita had a strong impact on the electoral support won by the presidential candidate of the incumbent party. These findings were then reported to George Shultz and John Erlichman in the fall of 1971.[24] (Of course attentive readers of Nixon's *Six Crises* already knew about the importance of economic factors in national elections.) Finally, the economic policies of 1971-1972 led to a fresh test and a reconfirmation of the proposition that good economic times benefit incumbents.

[24] Letter of April 25, 1977, from William A. Niskanen to Edward R. Tufte.

6
Macroeconomics under Conditions of Political Competition: Conclusions and Evaluations

As goes politics, so goes economic policy and performance. This is the case because as goes economic performance, so goes the election.

The regular, routine features of political life—the beliefs of politicians about the electorate, the timing of elections, the ideologies and platforms of political parties, and the location on the left-right spectrum of the political party controlling the government—are significant determinants of almost all important aspects of macroeconomic policy and performance. In particular, the timing of elections influences the rate of unemployment and growth in real disposable income, the short-term management of inflation and unemployment, the flow of transfer payments, the undertaking of expansionary or contractive economic policies, and the time perspective of economic policy-making. The platform of the political party controlling the government helps decide policies that determine the unemployment rate, the inflation rate, the size and rate of growth of central government, the extent of income equalization due to the tax system, taxing principles and practices, and social welfare activity.

Political life, then, is far more than an occasional random shock to a self-contained, isolated economic system; rather, economic life vibrates with the rhythms of politics.

The preceding chapters have described the motivations and apparatus involved in the political control of the economy and, further, provided some quantitative estimates of the strength of political-economic interconnections. To conclude, I will discuss the scope of political control over the national economy and the meaning of the findings for the making of competent, rational economic policy in a democracy.

LIMITS TO POLITICAL CONTROL

The fact that economic policy in a democracy is conducted in a competitive political environment has many consequences, both for the economy and for politics. Yet the influence of politicians, parties, and voters on macroeconomic outcomes is limited, checked by competing devices for making economic policy as well as by the forces that diminish the effectiveness of any method for systematically steering a large, open, diverse economy. The limits to political control include:

The private economy. Much economic activity transpires completely outside the scope of public control or even review. Belief in the private control of private property endures as a powerful and often dominant principle in the operating economic ideologies of capitalist democracies, particularly the United States. Public influence comes to bear on many economic sectors only when private enterprises seek public intervention to rescue them from adverse market outcomes or when the external costs of total private control become scandalous or publicly intolerable. Thus the political control of the economy often operates at the margin—a shift in the inflation rate here, a fluctuation in unemployment there—rather than on the underlying structure of the economy, public and private.

Incompetence. As a result of exogenous shocks, wars, structural changes, lack of understanding, and many other factors, large open economies may be very difficult to manage, regardless of whether the purpose is to win elections, to exert political priorities, or simply to moderate short-run economic fluctuations. Additionally, the electorate and even political platforms do not always send clear messages about the desirable course of action, or the desired goals may be impossible to achieve or inconsistent with one another.

Policy inertia and divided interests. When a number of agencies have to approve and act on economic policy, the

138

lead time may become long and uncertain. In implementing the three major tax bills of the 1960s, Congress delayed 18, 13, and 18 months. An econometric simulation judged two of the delays as costly and one as fortuitously beneficial.[1] It is only recently that the timing of the determination of the annual federal budget has been shaped up.[2] Mobilizing the central bank or the bureaucracy may prove difficult for the political leadership of a country. Despite the claims of political-economic models, there is no single cohesive unit called the "government" devoted to maximizing the incumbency of the executive. Legislatures, legislative committees, bureaucracies, agencies, central banks, and all the others involved in shaping economic outcomes all have quite different constituencies from the executive, and those constituencies may not be at all sympathetic to the economic program of the executive.

Mutual agreement to depoliticize. Some areas of economic management, by mutual agreement of the competing political parties, may be off limits to political control, at least in noncrisis times. One frequently mentioned example is the administration of the operations of central banks. Of course the rhetoric of depoliticalization is itself a political weapon, inspired by agencies seeking to prevent external political control and to permit them quietly to serve the interests of their own constituencies. The depoliticized economic agency may have a powerful constituency that protects it. It may seek the shelter of bipartisanship, successfully serving the interests of incumbents of all political parties. Or there may be widely agreed upon standards that would clearly be compromised by political control. The collection and reporting of economic data—such as the unemployment rate, which sometimes has major political significance—comes to mind as a depoliticized area, despite occasional reports of hanky-panky.[3] In

[1] Paul R. Portney, "Congressional Delays in U.S. Fiscal Policy-making," *Journal of Public Economics*, 5 (April-May 1976), 237-247.

[2] Mary Russell and David S. Broder, "Hill's Budget Power Survives Jolts from Outside and In," *Washington Post*, May 15, 1977, p. A3.

[3] Even the reporting of economic indicators has a complicated political history, involving White House intervention in statistical

general, unless there are external counterpressures from outside the government, the more important the agency or the issue, the more likely and intense the political control.

Economic theory. Whether Democratic or Republican, those economists who go to Washington to serve as high-level economic advisers arrive with the analytical and ideological baggage common to their discipline. The consensus of mainstream applied economics embraces an appreciation of opportunity costs, a high valuation placed on economic growth and efficiency as well as on maximizing productivity, an interventionist approach to macroeconomic stabilization, and belief in the virtues of the results turned out by free, competitive markets.[4] In overly simple terms, the economists'

---

agencies (in the Watergate tapes, Nixon engaged in a diatribe against the "Jew-boys" at the Bureau of Labor Statistics). See Philip M. Hauser, "Statistics in Politics," *The American Statistician,* 27 (April 1973), 69-71; and Eileen Shanahan, "Deciphering Politicized Economic Statistics," *New York Times,* October 22, 1972, p. IV-3. Because reported changes in economic indicators occasionally have political consequences (the good news generated by a pre-election drop in the unemployment rate, for example) and economic consequences (the movement of the stock market or other markets in response to government economic reports), the exact dates of monthly and quarterly publication of economic indicators are set years in advance (under Office of Management and Budget Circular A-76). Such a schedule provides a defense for agencies resisting White House pressure to accelerate the release of good news and delay bad news in relation to the election. These things can make a difference in a close election; an element in the Conservative defeat of the incumbent Labour party in the 1970 British elections was the last-minute shift in the vote induced (perhaps) by the highly unfavorable balance-of-trade figures published the weekend before the election. See Richard Rose, ed., "The Polls and the 1970 Election," Occasional Paper Number 7, Survey Research Centre, University of Strathclyde, 1970.

[4] The consensus is described in Arthur M. Okun, *The Political Economy of Prosperity* (Washington, D.C.: The Brookings Institution, 1970), chapter 1. See also the American Economic Association presidential addresses of George J. Stigler, "The Economist and the State," *American Economic Review,* 55 (March 1965), 1-18; and Walter W. Heller, "What's Right with Economics," *American*

consensus combines a Democratic macroeconomic policy and a Republican microeconomic policy. The consensus extends to specific policy prescriptions: free trade, no floors or ceilings on prices and wages, and selective timing of federal spending to stabilize the ups and downs of the national economy. In the rough-and-tumble politics of economic policy, those prescriptions often lose out to the preferences of the special interest groups most affected by the policy at issue and also to the policies that help the president and the political parties build electoral coalitions, benefit friends, and punish enemies. Thus a frequent theme in reports of academic economists who serve as presidential advisers is the conflict between what they see as the optimal policy on grounds of technical efficiency and what is actually done after small but well-organized and powerful special interests have had their say politically.[5] The research literature on interest group politics verifies these reports, for the library shelves sag with accounts of the grubby victories won by textile manufacturers, television assemblers, airlines, maritime interests, farmers, oil companies, shoemakers, and a host of others.[6]

It is important to remember, however, that despite the frequent defeats of economic theory by politics, the professional

---

Economic Review, 65 (March 1975), 1-26; as well as the diversity of views in the first six essays in Ryan C. Amacher, Robert D. Tollison, and Thomas D. Willett, eds., *The Economic Approach to Public Policy* (Ithaca, N.Y.: Cornell University Press, 1976). George Stigler claims it is a consensus on conservative values in "The Politics of Political Economists," in his *Essays in the History of Economics* (Chicago: University of Chicago Press, 1965), pp. 51-65.

[5] Okun, *The Political Economy of Prosperity,* chapter 1; also informal reports from economists who have worked in the Ford and Carter administrations.

[6] Several recent reports have gone beyond the juicy stories of the case studies to look for more systematic relationships between economic power and its effect on legislative outcomes. See Lester M. Salamon and John J. Siegfried, "Economic Power and Political Influence: The Impact of Industry Structure on Public Policy," *American Political Science Review,* 71 (September 1977), 1026-1043; and J. J. Pincus, "Pressure Groups and the Pattern of Tariffs," *Journal of Political Economy,* 83 (August 1975), 757-778.

economic consensus has an institutionalized voice close to the president (in the Council of Economic Advisers) and, unlike other ideologies, an apparent intellectual authority deriving from a technical apparatus unfathomable to politicians.[7] In such an atmosphere, the policy prescriptions of the economists' consensus will influence economic policy and perhaps even compete with political considerations (the timing of elections, preferences of voters and interest groups, and party platforms) in making economic policy. With the modesty characteristic of claims of disciplinary relevance, George Stigler suggested in 1965—the heyday of the economics profession in public policy—that economists would exert increasing political power in service of the public good: "Our expanding theoretical and empirical studies will inevitably and irresistibly enter into the subject of public policy, and we shall develop a body of knowledge essential to intelligent policy formulation. And then, quite frankly, I hope that we become the ornaments of democratic society whose opinions on economic policy shall prevail."[8]

EVALUATION

We have seen what happens when macroeconomic policy is conducted under conditions of partisan political competition: to a significant degree, the economic priorities of the

---

[7] Presidents have not been blessed with great economic sophistication, if anecdote can serve as evidence. President Kennedy said that the way he remembered the difference between fiscal and monetary policy was that monetary and Martin (William McChesney Martin, then Chairman of the Federal Reserve) both began with M. President Nixon once pointedly expressed his distaste for extended briefings on foreign exchange problems, particularly those relating to the lira. See Leonard Silk, "Tapes' Insight on Nixon: They Indicate His Economic Thinking Is Heavily Weighted by Political Factors," *New York Times*, August 7, 1974, p. 42.

[8] Stigler, "The Economist and the State," p. 17. When asked what it was about the discipline of economics that led some to describe it as the "queen of the social sciences," Harold Lasswell reportedly suggested three reasons: (1) some theory, (2) an extensive body of data, often with a common unit of measurement, i.e., dollars, and (3) economists talk themselves up a lot.

party elected to run the government are carried out. This democratic control of economic outcomes is impressive, particularly when compared to the extent of such control for other issues, such as foreign policy. All the interconnections between the electorate, electoral outcomes, party platforms, and economic policy and performance simply do not operate with comparable strength for any other major issues dealt with by national governments. The climate of political competition, however, leads to some perverse outcomes in economic policy; the costs of the political control of the economy may be substantial. The electoral-economic cycle breeds a lurching, stop-and-go economy the world over. Governments fool around with transfer payments, making an election-year prank out of the social security system and the payroll tax. There is a bias toward policies with immediate, highly visible benefits and deferred, hidden costs—myopic policies for myopic voters. Special interests induce coalition-building politicians to impose small costs on the many to achieve large benefits for the few. The result is economic instability and inefficiency.

Given this mixed record, what conclusions should be reached concerning the quality of performance of the political-economic system described in the preceding chapters? What about reform?

Several economists, writing recently, have emphasized the costs of the political control of the economy and have advocated the depoliticization of economic policy. The proposed cures usually prescribe less control over economic policy by politicians and more control by economists.

One important line of argument in this reformist literature is that political control fails to achieve the objectively optimal economic path. All kinds of simple models can be constructed to make this point. For example, consider a new administration beginning its term when unemployment is high. Assume it has the instruments, the will, and the constituency to make it worthwhile to drive the unemployment rate down two percentage points over its four-year term. Neglecting all other factors (particularly trade-offs), the "public interest" path would be to get unemployment down as soon as possible

143

for as long as possible. But suppose the administration believes that the electorate responds to *changes* in the unemployment rate, that the "most important thing in practical politics is the direction which things are moving, rather than where they are. If they're static and bad, sure, then the guy in the White House is in a hell of a fix. But if the economy is prospering but not yet prosperous, if the trend is good, that's a bit more propitious."[9] Given such a model of how the electorate responds to changes in economic conditions, the electorally ideal path for the incumbent government is to move into the election with a falling rather than a flat unemployment rate. To oversimplify, the area between the two curves represents the social cost of an electorally inspired economic policy:

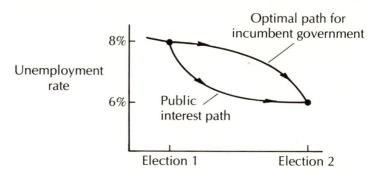

[9] Bryce Harlow, quoted in R. W. Apple, "President's Forecast: Gloomy Economic Assessment Gives G.O.P. Shudders About 1976 Election," *New York Times*, February 4, 1976, p. 17. Since the unemployment rate was 9 percent at the time—the highest in decades—almost any other theory of electoral behavior would have been awfully depressing. It is not surprising that elements of rationalization may enter into politicians' theories about how voters respond to economic conditions. Perhaps some of those theories are made to come true by the proper campaign strategy—by emphasizing in the campaign the rate of economic change rather than the long-run level of performance, by ignoring the disadvantageous aspects of economic performance, or by promoting other issues to the voters in order to deflect attention from the unhappy level of economic performance.

Additional assumptions about the tactics of politicians and the preferences of voters yield a similar conclusion that the demands of the electoral cycle prevent achievement of the optimal mix of economic policies. In an analysis that makes its heroic premises clear, Nordhaus claims that "the politically determined policy choice will have lower unemployment and higher inflation than is optimal."[10]

The suggestion that the electoral-economic cycle and, more generally, the political control of economic policy fail to produce the optimal economic path or the optimal mix of economic policies might be more persuasive if we knew what the optimum was, how to achieve it, and if a majority, say, of those affected would agree on the optimum and the methods for achieving it.[11] None of these things is going to happen in the real world, and so the argument is mainly that the unobtainable optimum is better than the real world, which we knew before we started. More realistically, the costs, if any, of pre-election economic stimulation might be estimated by simulations in macroeconomic models. This procedure might yield quantitative estimates of the inefficiencies caused by the electoral-economic cycle. One would expect that the pre-election binge of 1971-1972 was very costly; possibly in other election years, by contrast, the economic stimulation might have been quite justified on economic grounds (at least if we could agree on what those might be).

Another possible cost of the electoral-economic cycle in particular and the political control of the economy in general is the familiar suggestion that election-year economics promotes long-run inflation. Electoral pressure, it is argued, prevents "any sustained experiment either in running the econ-

[10] William D. Nordhaus, "The Political Business Cycle," *Review of Economic Studies*, 42 (April 1975), 185. An alternative result derives from alternative but equally plausible assumptions; see Bruno S. Frey and Hans-Jürgen Ramser, "The Political Business Cycle: A Comment," *Review of Economic Studies*, 43 (October 1976), 553-555.

[11] See Charles E. Lindblom, *The Intelligence of Democracy* (New York: The Free Press, 1965) and Edward C. Banfield, *Political Influence* (New York: The Free Press, 1960), chapter 12.

omy at a lower pressure of demand, or at a more constant pressure free of the ratchet effect of election booms."[12] In a similar vein:

> In my judgment, the 1972 overstimulation is much more serious than still another forecasting error because it is added evidence regarding the strong and inherently inflationary bias of virtually all modern governments. The bias is the result of a combination of factors which have increased the incentives and the technical means for governments to cause inflation at the same time that the constraints on their abilities to do so have been severely weakened. The bias increases in election years. For those in or close to the seats of state power, the costs of paying the piper fall sharply after a successful election day. The myopia of voters, including those with Ph.D.'s in economics, makes the game possible. Are we destined to add to our list a new cycle with a periodicity of four years?[13]

For the most part, this apparent inflationary bias must occur because voters are misled (failing to appreciate the post-election inflation resulting from the pre-election boom) rather than because voters are soft on inflation. According to the evidence, voters do not like inflation at all. During inflationary times, "high prices," "the cost of living," and "inflation" are named as the most important national problem in surveys of the electorate. Voters respond to changes in *real* disposable income. Kramer has reported data showing that when inflation is high the incumbent party does not fare well in national elections.[14] Indeed, since the political costs

[12] Samuel Brittan, *Steering the Economy* (LaSalle, Ill.: Open Court, 1971), p. 455. See also Paul McCracken, "Reflections on Economic Advising," delivered at Conference on Advising the President, Princeton University, October 31, 1975.

[13] David Meiselman, "The 1973 Report of the President's Council of Economic Advisers: Whistling in the Dark," *American Economic Review*, 63 (September 1973), 582.

[14] These findings are reported in the Bobbs-Merrill reprint (PS-498), containing data corrections, of Gerald H. Kramer, "Short-Term Fluctuations in U.S. Voting Behavior, 1896-1964," *American Political Science Review*, 65 (March 1971), 131-143.

of inflation may be greater than the political costs of unemployment, democratic governments may be overly tolerant of unemployment (that is, if we could know what the optimum might be). At any rate, the evidence hints that if voters were informed about phony election-year prosperity and the inflationary costs it entailed, they would take it into account in their voting decision. By supporting parties of the Right, voters can elect a government that will, if past experience is a guide, reliably reduce inflation. Thus the inflationary bias, if it exists at all, does not appear to develop out of an inherent, structural defect in the democratic political arrangement under which elected politicians exert significant control over economic policy in response to the mandate of the electorate.

Another complaint against the political control of the economy is that it may discourage long-range planning by creating a quick-fix, crisis mentality in economic policy formulation. Paul McCracken's statement exemplifies the tensions felt by economic advisers who must operate within a democratic political system:

A more fundamental problem is that the whole process of economic policy decision-making has such a short-run focus. To some extent this is deeply embedded in the political calendar. The year following a Presidential election is the most important in the quadrennial cycle for major actions. Those elected have received a mandate. The next year all members of the House and one-third of the Senate face an off-year election. The next year is the year before the next Presidential election—when many in the House and all in the Senate are running for President. Indeed, an inadequately recognized aspect of the Watergate tragedy is that it lost for us the best of the four years in this election cycle.

In any case this political calendar does not mesh well with the time required for economic processes to work themselves out. This makes for disinterest in programs with a pay-off beyond one or two years. And it creates a

147

great temptation to embrace programs that in the short run might be popular even if they are inimical to the longer-run economic vitality of the country.[15]

Part of the short-run focus is special to economic policy. Economic forecasts are not much good beyond a year or two at most and so long-range planning may be idle, swamped by the need (often the political need, to be sure) to respond to short-term economic fluctuations.[16] In contrast, some non-economic programs have a planned pay-off that comes gradually over many years. (Consider the major governmental initiatives of the 1960s: the space program, civil rights legislation, extension of social welfare, the war in Vietnam, and monitoring of domestic dissent.)

It is true, however, that the electoral calendar—and the time perspective used by voters in judging how well the incumbent administration is doing in managing the economy—significantly influences the time horizon of economic policy. Although some structure for long-range economic policy

[15] "Reflections on Economic Advising." This statement reveals the fascination and hostility toward politics of high-level economic advisers, a conflict induced by trying to perform for both the president and for one's professional colleagues. These issues are discussed by former economic advisers in "How Political Must the Council of Economic Advisers Be?" *Challenge*, 17 (March-April 1974), 28-42; see also Hugh Heclo, "OMB and the Presidency—The Problem of 'Neutral Competence,'" *The Public Interest*, 38 (Winter 1975), 80-98.

[16] "For instance, during the interval 1971:3 to 1974:4 the root mean-square error of the Livingston panel of economists in forecasting the consumer price index six months ahead was 3.5 percentage points at an annual rate, compared with an error of 1.6 percentage points over the previous 17 years. Not only did the panel forecasters fail to predict the increased variance of the inflation rate in the 1970s, but also they fell far short in predicting the cumulative total price change between 1971 and 1976—24.0 percent compared with the actual change of 34.0 percent." Robert J. Gordon, "Can the Inflation of the 1970s be Explained?" *Brookings Papers on Economic Activity*, 1977:1, 253. A more general elaboration of this point is found in Robert A. Dahl and Charles E. Lindblom, *Politics, Economics, and Welfare* (New York: Harper & Row, 1953), pp. 300-301.

and priorities is provided by the platform and ideology of the governing political party, the president's attention is regularly diverted from putatively noble long-range goals to the low politics involved in winning re-election. If there is a price to be paid here, it is the price we pay for having elections. The only worse situation would be if political leaders did not have to worry about elections at all.[17]

Are the election-year economic machinations described in Chapters 1 and 2 completely undesirable? I am not sure. At a minimum the issue is more subtle than the anti-political evaluation now recorded in the economic and reformist literature. One relevant observation is that election-year economics may tend to redistribute income downwardly. A bribe to the voters is, after all, a bribe to the voters. In election years, unemployment drops, social welfare programs expand, and beneficiary payments to millions of people increase. The months before the election are the "liberal hour," replacing the administration's efforts earlier in the term to build "business confidence." There appears to be a tendency for an administration to broaden the scope of its economic patronage as the course of its term in office moves closer toward the upcoming election. My conclusion is that an assessment of the electoral-economic cycle significantly depends on how one evaluates the specific policies advanced by the cycle. Or perhaps the electoral-economic cycle should be accepted as one of the externalities and inefficiencies resulting from the democratic—and consequently political—control of economic policy.

What are the options? Most of the proposed reforms seek to reduce the scope of political control of the economy, sometimes replacing politicians with economists. The proposals include:

—entrusting "economic policy to persons who will not be tempted by the Sirens of partisan politics. . . . A similar

[17] These issues are examined with particular clarity ("the best security for the fidelity of mankind is to make their interest coincide with their duty") in Hamilton's discussion of the president's eligibility for re-election in *Federalist Papers* 71 and 72.

possibility is to turn fiscal policy over to a Treasury dominated by civil servants."[18]

—"experiments with 'depoliticization' of some policy agencies, such as the central bank."[19]

—"a more liberal use of discretionary powers of the cabinet without previous consent of parliament."[20]

Some other proposed remedies for the electoral-economic cycle are ingenious but impractical. One idea is to reduce the flexibility of incumbents to determine the timing of elections in those countries without fixed election dates; and "a theoretical possibility would be to let the exact time of elections be determined by a random process."[21]

The remedies of depoliticization would do more than thwart those seeking a short-run economic kicker right before the election; the remedies dilute the overall political management of the economy, giving the civil service and economists a stronger role in economic policy choices. Depoliticization is seen as good: "It is interesting to note that monetary policy is generally less closely controlled by representative bodies than is fiscal policy. Since monetary policy is central to allocation over time, this may be more desirable than is usually supposed."[22]

For the broader depoliticization proposals to work, the electorate is also going to have to be depoliticized, and told to stop holding incumbent politicians responsible for the state of the economy. It is hard to ask politicians to give up influence over economic policy if they are going to be held responsible for economic performance.

Part of the contemporary disgust with political influences

[18] Nordhaus, "The Political Business Cycle," p. 188.

[19] Assar Lindbeck, "Stabilization Policy in Open Economies with Endogenous Politicians," *American Economic Review*, 66 (May 1976), 18. The political model underlying the economic policy preference for a depoliticized central bank is discussed in John T. Woolley, "The Politics of Central Banking: Comparisons from Recent Experience," paper delivered at the annual meeting of the American Political Science Association, September 1977.

[20] Lindbeck, "Stabilization Policy," p. 18.

[21] Ibid., n. 8.

[22] Nordhaus, "The Political Business Cycle," p. 188, n. 2.

on the formation of economic policy is more a short-run product of the times than anything else. The skepticism—and the research literature—concerning the political control of the economy developed only after the economic boom of the Nixon re-election campaign, the world-wide election boom that year, and the consequent inflation of 1973. To turn round Keynes' famous remarks:

> The ideas of politicians, both when they are right and when they are wrong, are more powerful than is commonly understood. Indeed the world is ruled by little else. Economists, who believe themselves exempt from any political influences, are usually the slave of some defunct politician. Academic scribblers, who hear voices in the air, are distilling their frenzy from some madman in authority a few years back.[23]

I reach the following conclusions about the depoliticization remedies. First, the proposed remedies are too obtuse, removing economic policy from political control in general, all in an effort to cure the particular problem of election-year economics. Second, the proposed remedies would significantly reduce the electorate's control over that one area—economic policy—where the democratic model actually seems to be most realized in practice.[24]

Other than pursuing the crude remedies of depoliticization, what might be done to reduce the probability that gov-

[23] What Keynes actually wrote was: ". . . the ideas of economists and practical philosophers, both when they are right and when they are wrong, are more powerful than is commonly understood. Indeed the world is ruled by little else. Practical men, who believe themselves exempt from any intellectual influences, are usually the slave of some defunct economist. Madmen in authority, who hear voices in the air, are distilling their frenzy from some academic scribbler of a few years back. *The General Theory of Employment, Interest and Money* (New York: Harcourt, Brace, 1936), pp. 383-384.

[24] Although their faith in the democratic control of the economy is limited—"budgets cannot be left adrift in the sea of democratic politics"—Buchanan and Wagner display greater sensitivity than most reformers to reconciling democratic control with reforms in economic management. See James M. Buchanan and Richard E. Wagner, *Democracy in Deficit* (New York: Academic Press, 1977).

ernments will pursue a corrupt and politically manipulative economic policy? Some reforms should deal with the specific techniques of quick-and-dirty economics employed in past elections; other reforms, however, should cut more deeply to the underlying cause by seeking to reduce the electoral advantages accruing from a politically manipulative economic policy. In particular:

Desynchronization of economic and electoral calendars. Some of the destabilizing effects of the electoral-economic cycle can be reduced by greater governmental and public attention to how calendars regulate the flow of government spending so that such calendars (as well as start-up dates for payment increases) are neutral or even counter-cyclical with respect to the electoral calendar.[25]

Pressure on collaborators. The public harassment of those agencies (see Chapter 2) most contributing to the pre-election heaping of transfer payments might reduce the election-year tendency to do some of December's business in October and November. Public criticisms for past sins give agencies an incentive for not accommodating the president's re-election campaign in the future.[26]

Special attention to re-election campaigns. One of the gravest threats to a rational economic policy arises when an

[25] As I indicated in Chapter 2, beginning the new fiscal year in October is a step in the wrong direction. Would it be too radical to have the fiscal year match the calendar year?

[26] Two of the most electorally rhythmic transfer programs, social security and veterans benefits (from which more than half the electorate receives payments), are also programs for which members of Congress do much rewarding casework for their constituents who are having trouble with the Washington bureaucracy. Such district servicing—in which the representative's staff takes up a constituent's difficulties (usually in getting a check) with the government agency— makes a contribution to the electoral survival of incumbent members of Congress. See Morris P. Fiorina, *Congress: Keystone of the Washington Establishment* (New Haven: Yale University Press, 1977).

incumbent president seeks re-election. Although some incumbents have gone further than others in accelerating the pre-election economy, the effect of a re-election campaign on the economy has almost always been a strong one. The growth rate of real disposable income during years when an incumbent president sought re-election has typically been double that of other years. Bureaucratic resistance to economic manipulation is low during re-election campaigns. The reasons are obvious. Political appointees want to stay in office. Furthermore, the incumbent president will usually win (Ford was the only exception since Hoover) and, with the campaign over, be able to settle scores with those who did not help out sufficiently. Knowing this, many help out. The economic exuberance induced by re-election campaigns can be tempered by the particularistic remedies of desynchronization and pressure on collaborators. Probably more important, however, is the global remedy of public exposure.

Public exposure of the political manipulation of the economy. Two of the biggest mistakes of recent economic policy came about as presidents pursued covert economic policies with concealed priorities. A perverse policy replaced economic good sense in both

— the cover-up of the cost and postponement of the financing of the Vietnam war from 1965 to 1967 and
— the all-out stimulation of the economy for the 1972 re-election campaign.[27]

27 Covert financing is extensive in spite of the constitutional command that "a regular statement and account of the receipts and expenditures of all public money shall be published from time to time" and in spite of other legislation requiring full disclosure. On covert financing (including Vietnam), see Louis Fisher, *Presidential Spending Power* (Princeton: Princeton University Press, 1975), chapter 9. The Vietnam period is also discussed in Okun, *The Political Economy of Prosperity*, chapter 3. The "McCracken Report" notes that "the Administration did not seek a temporary tax surcharge until 1967, and it was not enacted until June 1968. This delay in adopting fiscal measures to neutralise rising defence outlays provides one of the most striking examples of the difficulties encountered when

These actions (along with the increase in the price of oil) are probably responsible for much of the inflation and economic disruption of the 1970s. In both cases, the highest economic priority of the president and the plans to achieve it failed to emerge as a public, political issue. There was, in fact, deliberate concealment of the economic agenda by the White House, a lack of testing of economic priorities in the political marketplace, and a unilateral course of policy undertaken by the president and his economic advisers. The mistakes were not made because gluttonous voters were possessed with "inflationary bias," or because of "voter myopia" (except insofar as politicians failed to reveal their economic priorities), or because of an excess of democracy in economic policy-making. Quite the contrary. The operating assumption made by those who undertook and secretly pursued these mistaken policies was, I believe, absolutely correct: sleazier efforts at manipulating economic policy for short-run advantage cannot survive public scrutiny. Since the incumbent administration cannot be relied upon to reveal such manipulations, a special responsibility falls upon the political opposition—the out-party—to expose myopic economic policies. It also falls upon those who write about national economics. That responsibility is to improve the level of public understanding so that voters can evaluate and repudiate corrupt economic policies.[28] Such a remedy—of which this book is a part—would strengthen the already functioning linkages between the preferences of citizens and the determination of economic policy and performance.

---

the needs of demand management conflict with perceived requirements of social policy or 'political necessity'" (from the OECD report, *Towards Full Employment and Price Stability* [Paris, June 1977], p. 47). Somewhat in the tradition of the reformist literature discussed earlier, the volume provides a useful analysis of the political economy of the 1970s.

[28] Public exposure also limits the success of special interests in their efforts to induce the government to impose small costs on the many to achieve large benefits for the few.

Appendix: Data Sources

TABLE 1-1. Computed from yearly data for elections, disposable income, price changes, and population for the 27 countries. The real disposable income figures per capita were obtained by dividing disposable income by yearly population for each year, with that result then adjusted by the price index (1963 baseline) to yield real disposable income per capita. The election year is coded as being in year X if the date of the election falls between June of year X and May of year $X + 1$. Election dates for the major national elections (usually for the lower house of parliament and for president in those countries where that office is politically important) are from *Deadline Data on World Affairs*, McGraw Hill Publications (Greenwich, Connecticut: McGraw Hill, various dates); *Political Handbook and Atlas of the World, 1970*, Richard P. Stebbins and Alba Amoia, eds. (New York: Simon and Schuster, 1970); and Thomas T. Mackie and Richard Rose, *The International Almanac of Electoral History* (London: Macmillan & Co., 1974). The type of disposable income data varies from source to source. From the OECD books listed below, I used disposable income of households and private nonprofit institutions serving households. From the U.N. sources, national disposable income was obtained, which the 1970 edition describes as "the net receipts of residents from employment, entrepreneurship and property, and unrequited current transfers." Disposable income for India, New Zealand, and Norway are all private disposable income and for Israel, private disposable income from domestic sources.

In compiling such a table, dozens of arbitrary decisions are involved. I had two independent compilations made; the first yielded 21 out of 27 countries and the second 19 out of 27 countries that displayed a bias for election-year economic acceleration. Another replication, for the 7 largest capitalist countries over a longer period of time with a different economic indicator, is reported in Chapter 3. Several case studies, cited in Chapter 1, supplement the aggregated results of Table 1-1.

The following list contains the basic data sources, which were supplemented in a few cases by national statistical yearbooks.

For population data:

Demographic Yearbook 1962, Statistical Office of the United Nations, Department of Economic and Social Affairs, New York, 1963; Table 4, pp. 130-141.

Demographic Yearbook 1965, Statistical Office of the United Nations, Department of Economic and Social Affairs, New York, 1966; Table 4, pp. 128-139.

Demographic Yearbook 1970, Statistical Office of the United Nations, Department of Economic and Social Affairs, New York, 1971; Table 4, pp. 126-135.

Demographic Yearbook 1972, Statistical Office of the United Nations, Department of Economic and Social Affairs, New York, 1973; Table 4, pp. 140-146.

For data on disposable income:

National Accounts of OECD Countries, 1950-1968, Organization of Economic Cooperation and Development.

National Accounts of OECD Countries, 1960-1971, Organization of Economic Cooperation and Development.

Yearbook of National Accounts Statistics, 1970, Statistical Office of the United Nations, Department of Economic and Social Affairs, New York, 1972.

Yearbook of National Accounts Statistics, 1971, Statistical Office of the United Nations, Department of Economic and Social Affairs, New York, 1973.

Yearbook of National Accounts Statistics, 1972, Statistical Office of the United Nations, Department of Economic and Social Affairs, New York, 1974.

For the consumer price index:

Statistical Yearbook 1967, Statistical Office of the United Nations, Department of Economic and Social Affairs, New York, 1968; Table 177, pp. 535-541.

Statistical Yearbook 1973, Statistical Office of the United Nations, Department of Economic and Social Affairs, New York, 1974; Table 173, pp. 542-548.

International Financial Statistics, International Monetary Fund, December 1969, vol. 22, no. 12, p. 31.

International Financial Statistics, International Monetary Fund, June 1973, vol. 26, no. 6, p. 35.

FIGURE 1-1. Computed from *The Annual Report of the Council of Economic Advisers* (Washington, D.C.: U.S. Government Printing Office, 1977), p. 213. (Cited hereafter as *CEA Report*.)

FIGURE 1-2. From *CEA Reports*, 1946-1977.

TABLE 1-2. Ibid.

TABLE 1-3. Computed from *CEA Report*, 1977, p. 213. Results comparable to those in this table are obtained when the absolute second difference (acceleration or deceleration in real disposable income) is used.

TABLE 2-1. From various monthly issues of the *Social Security Bulletin* (Washington, D.C.: U.S. Department of Health, Education, and Welfare) and from the *Social Security Bulletin: Annual Statistical Supplement*, 1973 and 1974.

FIGURE 2-1. The number of social security beneficiaries receiving the letter of October 1972 is reported in Executive Session Hearings, Senate Select Committee on Presidential Campaign Activities, *Presidential Campaign Activities of 1972* (Washington, D.C.: U.S. Government Printing Office, 1974), book 19, p. 9140. Copy of letter from Social Security Administration.

FIGURE 2-2. *CEA Reports*, 1972-1975.

FIGURE 2-3. *CEA Reports*, 1963-1977.

FIGURES 2-4 AND 2-5. Monthly issues of *Economic Indicators* (Washington, D.C.: U.S. Government Printing Office), 1962-1976.

FIGURE 2-6. Envelope from Social Security Administration.

FIGURE 2-7. *CEA Reports*, 1972-1975.

TABLE 2-2. Computed from *CEA Report*, 1976; 1946 data from *Economic Indicators*, January 1954.

TABLE 3-1. Computed from Agency for International Development, *Gross National Product: Growth Rates and Trend Data* (Washington, D.C.: May 1974); 1975 and 1976 data are estimates based on OECD data.

FIGURE 3-1. Mackie and Rose, *The International Almanac of Electoral History*, and newspaper reports.

FIGURE 4-1. Based on the election studies conducted at the Survey Research Center, University of Michigan, as reported in Arthur H. Miller and Warren E. Miller, "Partisanship and Performance: 'Rational' Choice in the 1976 Presidential Elections," paper delivered at the annual meeting of the American Political Science Association, September 1977.

FIGURE 4-2. Douglas Hibbs, Jr., "Political Parties and Macroeconomic Policy," *American Political Science Review*, 71 (December 1977), 1467-1487.

FIGURE 4-3. Computed from Hibbs, "Political Parties," and Malcolm Sawyer, "Income Distribution in OECD Countries," *OECD Economic Outlook: Occasional Studies*, July 1976, 3-36.

TABLE 4-1. Counts based on the text of the platforms supplied by the National Committees of the two parties.

TABLES 4-2, 4-3, AND 4-4. *The Economic Report of the President* and the CEA *Annual Report* have had the same format since the first Kennedy reports in January 1962; before that time, differing formats were used. In the counts, only five uses of either *inflation* or *unemployment* were counted *per page* of text in the reports (in order to trim outliers resulting from a single page or two). The counts reported here are surely undercounts, because it is easy to skip over the use of the counted words in the thousands of pages of text that were reviewed. The counts for several reports were independently replicated and also repeated; this procedure indicates that the undercount runs between 2 percent and 10 percent for each report. The undercounts that I did detect did not affect the substance of the results in any way. The economic data in Table 4-2 are from *CEA Reports*, 1976-1977.

TABLE 4-5. The NBC "Street Poll" interviewed nearly 15,000 voters at the polls on election day in randomly selected precincts. The survey was reasonably accurate on the major validity test, the presidential vote, running 53 percent for Carter. In most cases, other surveys (the Gallup Poll and the University of Michigan Survey Research Center election studies) have replicated the results of the NBC survey.

FIGURE 4-4. Computed from Hibbs, "Political Parties," and *The OECD Observer*, February 1974.

FIGURE 4-5. From David R. Cameron, "Open Economies, Electoral Politics, and the Expansion of the Public Economy: A Comparative Analysis," Yale University, manuscript, 1977.

FIGURE 4-6. *CEA Report*, 1977.

TABLES 5-1 AND 5-2; FIGURE 5-1. Votes computed from Donald E. Stokes and Gudmund Iversen, "National Totals of Votes Cast for Democratic and Republican Candidates for the U.S. House of Representatives, 1866-1960," Survey Research Center, University of Michigan, July 1962; from *Congressional Directories* (Washington, D.C.: U.S. Government Printing Office, yearly editions); and from *The Statistical Abstract of the United States* (Washington, D.C.: U.S. Government Printing Office, yearly editions). Not all sources agree on the overall vote totals (usually the differences between sources are less than 0.5 percent) because of different conventions for handling the vote cast in uncontested elections. Presidential approval from *The Gallup Opinion Index*, 64 (October 1970) and the *New York Times*, October 24, 1974. See also Edward R. Tufte, "Determinants of the Outcomes of Midterm Congressional Elections," *American Political Science Review*, 69 (September 1975), 812-826. Yearly change in real disposable income per capita computed from *CEA Report*, 1977.

TABLES 5-2, 5-3, 5-4, 5-5, AND 5-6; FIGURES 5-2 AND 5-3. Ibid. The data on net candidate advantage from 1952 to 1972 are based on Michael R. Kagay and Greg A. Caldeira, " 'I Like the Looks of His Face': Elements of Electoral Choice, 1952-1972," paper delivered at the annual meeting of the American Political Science Association, September 1975, except that these figures are for all those surveyed and that the 1972 computations are based on all five interviewee responses rather than on the three normally coded. These data were made available by Michael R. Kagay and Arthur H. Miller. Miller also provided the 1976 data. For 1948, I computed the net candidate advantage from the Inter-University Consortium for Political Research data tape, "The 1948 Minor Election Study," Angus Campbell and

161

Robert L. Kahn, principal investigators. Questions 35 and 36 were used. Although there are substantial differences between the 1948 survey and the 1952-1972 surveys, several tests indicate that our computations of the 1948 net candidate advantage resulted in a sensible number.

TABLE 5-7. Data for 1968 and 1972 (voters only) computed from data tape for election studies of the Survey Research Center, University of Michigan. Data for 1976 from NBC poll are described in notes for Table 4-5 (all those interviewed voted).

TABLE 5-8. NBC poll; see notes for Table 4-5.

Index

Library of Congress Cataloging in Publication Data

Tufte, Edward R., 1942-
  Political control of the economy.

  Includes index.
  1. Economic policy.   2. Macroeconomics.
3. Political science.   I. Title.
HB73.T83   338.9   77-85570
ISBN 0-691-07594-8